CERES

MORAY HOUSE INSTITUTE
THE UNIVERSITY OF E
CHARTERIS 2.4 &5   HOL
EDINBURGH EH8 8AQ

TEL: 0131 651 6371   FAX: 0131 651 6511
E-MAIL: ceres@ed.ac.uk

Centre for Education
for Racial Equality in
Scotland

00654716

Educ/L

SUPPORTING BILINGUAL LEARNERS IN SCHOOLS

CERES

MORAY HOUSE INSTITUTE OF EDUCATION
THE UNIVERSITY OF EDINBURGH
CHARTERIS 2.4 &5   HOLYROOD CAMPUS
EDINBURGH EH8 8AQ

TEL: 0131 651 6371   FAX: 0131 651 6511
E-MAIL: ceres@ed.ac.uk

Centre for Education
for Racial Equality in
Scotland

SUPPORTING BILINGUAL LEARNERS IN SCHOOLS

Maggie Gravelle

Trentham Books

First published in 1996 by Trentham Books Limited

Trentham Books Limited
Westview House
734 London Road
Oakhill
Stoke-on-Trent
Staffordshire
England ST4 5NP

© Maggie Gravelle 1996

All rights reserved. No part of this publication may be reproduced in any
material from (including photocopying or storing it in any medium by electronic
means and whether or not transiently or incidentally to some other use of this
publication) without the prior written permission of the copyright owner, except
in accordance with the provision of the Copyright, Designs and Patents Act 1988
or under the terms of a licence issued by the copyright Licensing Agency, 90
Tottenham Court Road, London W1P 9HE. Applications for the copyright
owner's written permission to reproduce any part of this publication should be
addressed in the first instance to the publisher.

British Cataloguing in Publication Data
A catalogue record for this book is available from the British Library
ISBN: 1 85856 053 5

Designed and typeset by Trentham Print Design Ltd., Chester
and printed in Great Britain by Bemrose Shafron (Printers) Ltd, Chester.

Contents

This book owes its existence to the pupils, of all ages and
many backgrounds, whom I have met and worked with.
They have taught me to watch and listen in order to
discover the delights and complexities of learning.
Maggie Gravelle, June 1996

Chapter 1

Entitlement and Provision

The number of bilingual learners in our schools is growing. This is partly due to an increased awareness on the part of education authorities, schools and individual teachers of the existence of different languages and therefore recognition of the bilingualism that already exists in their classrooms. Bilingual pupils who are fluent in English and have spent all their educational lives in an English medium school have knowledge and experience of language use that is at last being recognised. The rhetoric that proclaims bilingualism as an asset, although not realised in any practical sense within the curriculum other than through the acquisition of an extra GCSE to add to the league tables, is at least revealing the vast expertise of our bilingual community.

In addition the importance of building on children's experiences, long a component of learning theory, is starting to include language as an important element. Teachers, concerned particularly about the refugees and new arrivals with limited English fluency, are also earnest in their desire to meet the needs of all their pupils.

This, together with the imminent reduction in the number of specialist support teachers and the presence of bilingual learners in the mainstream rather than hidden in language centres or withdrawal groups, has led to the need for clear, practical advice, firmly grounded in theory. Teachers who are asking what they need to do and how it should be done deserve straightforward answers. They also need to understand the reasons behind the practice so that they can develop strategies and responses for themselves. We need to link the growing body of research about bilingualism and factors which affect success in the learning environment with the pedagogical questions that practitioners are asking.

Entitlement

The National Curriculum provides for the first time an entitlement to a `balanced and broadly based' curriculum which 'is also relevant to his or her particular needs' (DES, 1989). This entitlement is restricted, of course, to pupils in maintained schools 'i.e county and voluntary schools, special schools not established in a hospital and grant-maintained schools' (DES, 1989). But the phrase 'relevant to his or her particular needs' is one that has often been overlooked in discussions about what constitutes a broad and balanced curriculum.

What this entitlement means in reality is rather vague. According to the Parent's Charter it means, 'You have a right to a good education for your child. This means that you have a right to expect the school to do its best to make sure every child does as well as he or she possibly can.' (*Our Children's Education*, DFE, 1994). Questions such as what constitutes a 'good education' and how the school decides whether or not the child is doing as well as 'he or she possibly can' are left open.

Ministers and government officials have insisted that it is not the intention of SCAA or the government to define how the curriculum is to be taught. The chief measure of success in attaining the entitlement is to be through SATs and teacher assessment. Teachers and LEA advisors have spent many hours in meetings and training sessions deciding how the latest documents are to be interpreted and implemented. Meanwhile, Ofsted continue the round of school inspections and continue to identify success and failure in terms of quality of teaching and learning. School improvement research tells us that vision, leadership, collegiality, high expectations, diagnostic record-keeping and parental involvement are among the indicators of effective schools. (see for example, Mortimore et al, 1988, Smith and Tomlinson, 1989 and OFSTED, 1993)

Many views and opinions are being sought but the voice that is largely missing from the literature and directives is that of and on behalf of the ethnic minority and bilingual pupils.

The new National Curriculum makes the merest token acknowledgement of the existence of bilinguals, apart from those that speak Welsh, in our schools, despite strenuous representations from a number of bodies and individuals at the consultation stage. For example NALDIC (National Association for Language Development in the Curriculum) argued for:

> explicit guidance on using the time released by the slimmed down National Curriculum to provide learning opportunities for bilingual pupils where appropriate;

> systematic reporting of bilingual pupils' achievement in their first language and in English;

> the need to produce tests which are culturally friendly, explicit in terms of the task to be performed and conceptually clear as to the distinction between content, knowledge and skills and attendant language use. (Leung, 1994)

The Parent's Charter was translated into nine 'ethnic community languages'. This at least acknowledges the existence of languages other than English in which populations are literate, although it is interesting to note that Welsh is not considered an 'ethnic community language'. However, the existence and daily use of languages other than English in sections of the population seems not to have penetrated the National Curriculum.

Ofsted have recently revised the *Framework for the Inspection of Schools* so that Equal Opportunities is no longer a separate category but is integrated more centrally 'by making direct reference to these issues and establishing specific reporting requirements' (OFSTED, 1995). If entitlement is to be a reality then equality of opportunity needs to be explicit and at the forefront of all that inspectors do and report on, otherwise as experience has shown, it is all too easily lost completely. The proposals fall far short of full and explicit integration of equal opportunities at all levels. Indeed, the needs of bilingual pupils and issues which concern them, such as racial tension and harassment are given very little importance.

A recent Ofsted report on Educational Support for Minority Ethnic Communities (OFSTED, 1994) is based on visits to Section 11 projects during 1992/3. A comparison is made between classes with bilingual pupils but without Section 11 support and those where Section 11 support was available.

The report concludes that the need for specialist provision for bilingual pupils continues and it comments on the features that make provision effective. These include well planned and clearly structured work which motivates pupils, high teacher expectations, a suitable range of teaching and learning strategies, appropriate resources which are 'sensitive to children's cultural heritage' and good assessment and recording procedures.

School effectiveness research focuses largely on outcomes, in terms of measurement of learning success. Interest lies in the factors which produce a 'good school' and the claim is that a school with particular features is effective for all its pupils, of whatever background (see Smith and Tomlinson, 1989). A difficulty with this approach lies in the model that is being used. Some criteria of success must be decided upon, participant schools are then measured against these criteria and the researchers attempt to identify features which those that score well have in common. Success criteria must necessarily be easy to measure and compare across a wide range of different schools and populations. So far rather crude measures of success have been adopted and the value-added debate which merely argues for greater sophistication in these indicators, has not, yet, cleared the air. Again, the voice that is missing from much of this research is that of the participants. It might be interesting to investigate the success criteria that various members of the black and bilingual community identify.

So the 'particular needs' of bilingual learners have been addressed very inadequately by central government. Their views have not actively been sought and representations made by and on behalf of ethnic minority communities have largely been ignored.

Section 11

Since 1966, when the Local Government Act of that year was passed, successive governments have recognised that 'immigrant' communities have needs which have not been met in the mainstream. The legislation made it possible for the Home Secretary to give grants to local authorities who:

> in his opinion are required to make special provision in the exercise of any of their functions in consequence of the presence within their areas of substantial numbers of immigrants ...whose language or customs differ from those of the community (quoted in Dorn and Hibbert, 1987).

The intention of Section 11 of the 1966 Act was to provide for the multiplicity of needs of this community, but repeatedly a large proportion of the money has been granted to Education Authorities. Recently the monitoring and accountability for Section 11 grant spending has been improved and the application and reporting procedures made more rigorous. This, largely welcome and necessary, development has had the interesting effect of making providers more politically aware and vocal and the recently announced reduction in grant was vigorously opposed. The intention to absorb at least part of the Section 11 fund into the Single Regeneration Budget was postponed, at least for a few years.

However, the future is not secure. Changes over recent years in LEA powers and the determination of central government to devolve responsibility and financial control to schools, have made the provision of centrally managed Section 11 or SRB funded projects for the support of bilingual learners increasingly vulnerable. The recent identification within the GEST priorities of training mainstream teachers in meeting the needs of bilingual learners, is further indication of the trend to eliminate or at best reduce extra finance.

Many would argue that this is a necessary change. From the outset Section 11 was seen by some as divisive, an abrogation of responsibility on the part of mainstream educators and a palliative. It was certainly part of the assimilationist political philosophy of the time.

The history of changes in provision under Section 11 for bilingual learners has been related elsewhere (see for example Bourne, 1989 and Kecl, 1994). It is interesting to trace the changed view of support and curriculum need over the last few years in order to elucidate the trend towards reduction in special funding and the increasing devolvement to mainstream which seems to be current policy.

In the early days of Section 11 many children spent at least part of their week in off-site or separate 'Language Centres' where the emphasis was on rapid introduction to, and imparting of, English language skills. From the mid 1980s onwards, when both the Swann Report (DES, 1985) and the Calderdale report (CRE, 1986) pointed to the educational inadequacies and racism inherent in this style of education, there has been a change towards in-class support. In some cases this has merely been a form of withdrawal within the classroom, the specialist teacher working with a small group of bilingual learners in a corner of the room, but at its best it has operated on a team teaching model. This implies that although each teacher takes responsibility for a particular group of pupils, they plan jointly and share curricular aims. The Section 11 teacher has typically adapted and supplemented the mainstream material in order to make it more accessible to bilingual learners. The Section 11 teacher has also been responsible for the assessment and progression of bilingual learners in terms of their English language skills, and stages of progression were often devised in order to provide benchmarks (see Hester, 1993).

In terms of impact upon the curriculum the main effect has been an increase in multicultural education. Section 11 teachers, some of them from ethnic minority groups themselves, were often able to suggest a new perspective and to provide materials to support this. Where relationships between teachers are good and time allows it has had the effect of broadening the curriculum. More recently, the prescriptive and demanding nature of the National Curriculum, at least in its early versions, has militated against this breadth and the effects on the mainstream have perhaps diminished.

Partnership Teaching

The continued marginalisation of Section 11 teachers and of the pupils with whom they were associated has been a matter of concern and one response to this has been the development of partnership teaching. Partnership teaching differs from team teaching in that it is more firmly based within the institution and requires commitment in terms of policy and practice from the management. It also differs in the commitment it requires from the teaching partners. Not only do they take joint responsibility for planning, as is often the case in team teaching, but they share responsibility for the learning of the whole class. This may mean delegation, but through joint evaluation they are able to build a picture of the achievements and needs of all the pupils and can then plan to meet them.

This form of teaching has clear implications for both the language development of bilingual learners, which becomes part of the perspective of the mainstream teacher and not largely the concern of the Section 11 teacher, and for the relevance of the curriculum. The resourcing and organisational issues that are raised by this model of teaching should then be firmly on the whole school agenda.

As a way of developing and sharing teaching skills and perspectives partnership teaching has proved very successful. It is, however, expensive, long term and requires a degree of skill, knowledge and flexibility as well as commitment, which is not always available. Initial teacher training and INSET must also develop in ways which require and enable mainstream teachers to take responsibility for the language and learning of bilingual pupils. This will mean taking a fresh look at all areas of the school and its curriculum and developing a greater understanding of the place of languages within the learning process.

Mainstream teachers, many of whom have worked in constructive ways with Section 11 colleagues are, in a legal and practical sense, taking responsibility for the entitlement of all pupils to a relevant and challenging curriculum. They are also becoming increasingly aware of and sensitive to the needs of bilingual learners. Teachers in a wide range of schools in many parts of the country have bilingual learners in their classrooms. Many teachers are concerned that the pupils' right to full access to the curriculum is not always being met. And this is true of pupils that are relatively fluent in English as well as the new arrivals and refugees that create obvious and immediate demands on schools and teachers. Parents and ethnic minority communities are becoming more vocal in their demands for equality and teachers are anxious to respond.

Good practice

It is sometimes said that what is good practice for bilingual learners is good for all. At one level this is a reassuring statement which suggests that teachers will not be wasting their time nor that of their monolingual pupils if they provide a learning environment which is supportive to bilinguals. But in a number of other respects it becomes a bland and uninformative truism.

It has been used as an excuse for rather unspecific support which can lack either a language development focus or a curriculum development focus. For example, there are situations in both primary and secondary schools in which extra support is provided by teachers who are basically helping the bilingual learners to achieve the required outcome. The support then consists of helping the learner to understand and complete the particular task and providing the vocabulary that goes with it. The danger is that this has no impact on learning in the broader sense and does not equip the learner with a framework within which to become independent.

Alternatively the support can be almost entirely curriculum focused and concentrate on providing a rich, multicultural learning environment which allows bilinguals learner to incorporate their experiences and see themselves reflected in the material. While laudable in itself, this approach can leave the language development entirely to chance, relying more on peer support than on any analysis on the part of the teacher. Bilingual learners need both the curriculum that motivates and has relevance for them *and* the systematic language development and feedback that enables them to achieve within it.

What is seen as 'good practice' has changed over time and different teachers, parents and managements will interpret it in different ways. We therefore need to be very clear about what we mean by the term and what it in fact looks like in practice.

Alexander (1994) suggests that while the evidence for good practice is found in the classroom in the teaching methods, organisation, curriculum and relationships, it rests on the ideas and values which educators bring to the learning environment. The beliefs we have about what constitutes knowledge and how children learn will affect what happens in the classroom. Teachers also have views about child development and how to meet pupils' needs and these are set within a social and political context which influences decisions about curriculum choices, assessment strategies, parental involvement and so on.

Teachers do not always have time or opportunity to enter into these debates but all practice is influenced by views of learning, whether implicit or explicit. Often the presence of bilingual learners in our classrooms make us focus more intently on these issues.

Learning

The National Curriculum provides a statutory framework. There are increasing organisational and administrative pressures on teachers. In this situation there is a danger that provision for bilingual learners becomes piecemeal and tokenistic. This book is intended to raise questions but also to provide some answers. It is underpinned by theories of learning and of language acquisition which provide a framework and rationale for practical strategies. It is only by understanding 'why?' that we can really develop answers to 'how?' Practical tips and examples are useful only until they run out. Then we need to be able to develop strategies for ourselves.

Learning is a complex process. We are all doing it all the time on many different levels. We are using language to make sense of new experiences and fitting these to our existing understanding. We may need to adjust our explanations and we may need to reformulate our questions. We need others to help us to do this. We are using our language skills in a whole range of different contexts and for many different purposes. We all operate in several registers.

Bilingual learners are going through exactly the same processes. But for many the rate at which they are learning and the amount of new learning that they encounter is enormous. Much of this learning is taking place in and through a new language and without reference to their considerable existing skills in their first language. It may also be taking place at an age and in an environment which makes it stressful and difficult.

So all teachers need to have some understanding of the language acquisition process and how second language learning differs from learning the first language. They also need an understanding of the place of first language in education and what, even if they are monolingual teachers themselves, they can do to support its maintenance and development. They will want some reassurance and strategies for the educational and social involvement of bilingual learners in their classrooms, even when those children speak very little English. Once pupils become more fluent in their use of English the immediate need for extra support is less obvious. It is at this stage that learners are often left to manage as best they can and their achievement is affected. There are many ways in which teachers can continue to support these pupils' learning and language development.

Multicultural education is one approach to making the classroom a more welcoming environment for bilingual learners and reflecting the wider context more accurately. A relevant curriculum which challenges stereotypes and engages and motivates learners is a pre-requisite for learning.

There are many academic books which present the debates about theories and research into bilingualism and second language acquisition and a growing number which give detailed and analytical descriptions of the work of specialists teaching bilingual learners. My experience of working with mainstream teachers both during their initial training and on professional development courses suggests that they want some guidance as to 'how to do it themselves'. They may not have specialists to call on and learn from, but a growing number of them have bilingual learners, at all stages of language and learning, in their classrooms.

I have tried to indicate the thinking behind the strategies that are successful for bilingual learners so that, with some analysis, thought and preparation, mainstream colleagues can provide a suitable learning environment for all.

Chapter 2 looks at the language acquisition process and discusses the differences between first and second language development. It gives guidance on the most effective ways to support English language development. Chapter 3 raises the important issues around first language maintenance and development without which some learners can be seriously disadvantaged and makes recommendations about valuing and promoting languages and benefiting from linguistic diversity. Chapter 4 explores what bilingual learners bring to their learning and how to assess and meet their needs. Some practical suggestions are made or providing access to learning in the first few weeks

The issue of the curriculum is discussed in chapter 5. Its relevance increases pupils' interest and motivation to learn. The debate about multiculturalism and antiracism is argued and the effects that these views may have on classroom organisation and methodology discussed. The final chapter discusses questions of policy and practice and how these might be linked and makes suggestions about how to start the process of change and development in classrooms and schools.

Terminology

When Section 11 was first introduced and teachers needed to talk about the pupils they worked with, a number of different terms were used. The legislation referred to 'immigrants', reflecting the current political perspective. However, in education the term 'learners of English as a Second Language' became current, in part acknowledging the fact that not all the pupils concerned were first generation immigrants. In addition the term recognised that pupils already had a first language upon which they were building. Courses in Teaching English as a Second Language were offered and pupils and their teachers were referred to as ESL.

Gradually the terminology began to change as the importance and status of the first language was emphasised. From their earliest introduction to an English speaking environment pupils are beginning to develop an understanding of a language different from the one they have grown up with. The term 'bilingual' was increasingly used to show recognition of this developing skill. Like many terms it is used by different people in different ways and is open to misinterpretation. It fails to acknowledge the multilingual abilities possessed by many members of the community. It also appears to encompass all levels of fluency.

The academic literature includes detailed discussion of the terminology. Some writers have dealt with issues of fluency by introducing terms such as complete, ideal or balanced bilingual, semi-lingual and even double semi-lingual (see for example Beardsmore, 1982 for a full discussion of definitions and typologies). There have extensive debates about the views of bilingualism that are contained within these definitions. Grosjean (1985) Edelsky et al (1983) and Martin-Jones and Romaine (1986) argue that they betray a negative or deficit perception that has affected research and practice. Bilinguals are not simply two monolinguals in one body. They are unique and competent language users who have developed and are developing communicative competence, both receptive and productive, in the variety of situations in which they operate. Bilinguals should not be judged in terms of idealised and static views of language, nor should their proficiency be based on discrete, inappropriate tests which have relevance, if any, to monolingual language users.

We are all, in whatever language or languages we speak, developing in our ability to use and make meaning in a variety of situations and there is not one of us who could not become, or is not de-skilled in certain circumstances. In this context it is hard to see what a complete, ideal bilingual or monolingual might look like.

Because of the apparently all-embracing and misleading nature of the term 'bilingual' some educators are beginning to use 'English as an additional language user', abbreviated to EAL. This has the benefit of recognising that there are one or more languages in which the learner is already fluent and that English is being added to them. It makes no assumptions about the degree of fluency in English. However, to reduce individuals to ciphers, such as EAL, seems de-personalising, though not as bad as the unfortunate term LEPs, (limited English proficiency) used at one time in the USA. Will they become 'EALs' or 'SEALs', speakers of English as an additional language?

The term bilingual or bilingual learner will be used in this book to refer to pupils who have access on a regular basis to more than one language. This access may be a receptive understanding of a language that is used with a limited number of family members or it may imply a high level of fluency and literacy in several languages used in different contexts. In the cases of most bilinguals to whom the term is applied in this book, their skills and abilities in English and in their other languages are changing and developing. The use of the term bilingual implies the recognition that language use and the contexts for it differ and that these will need to be defined and described for each individual.

Home, community or first language are also problematic terms and all can be inaccurately applied. Heritage language and mother tongue have also been used, usually to refer to languages other than English. In the context of education it is sometimes helpful to refer to 'preferred language' since that indicates the language in which the pupil can best operate in the particular situation. However it carries with it different information and there is still a need for an agreed term. The 'home language' may be only one, and perhaps not even the predominant language of the home. The same is true of 'community language' and needs further clarification as to the community and context, disguising the fact that for many people several languages are used depending on the situation, for example whether in the mosque, with close family or in the wider community. 'Mother tongue' suggests that it was learnt from the mother and is certainly misleading in referring to families where the parents come from different language backgrounds. 'Heritage language' may carry the implication of ancient, even dead, languages and 'first language' if used literally is not necessarily the language most widely used by a pupil now. Many of the terms also suggests that the pupil operates in only one language other than English.

Dodson (1985) and Mills (1993) amongst others, use the term 'preferred language' to refer to the language that a speaker uses in any particular context. As a descriptive term this is helpful. It acknowledges the importance of social and psychological factors and also the varied use of a number of languages in different contexts. For educational purposes however, it has several disadvantages. It is important to record and inform teachers about the language and dialect skills that the pupil and his/her family actually have so that schools can respond appropriately. Dodson points out that preferred language, 'does not relate to an individual's preference for, or desire to use, one particular language rather than another' (p.327), so that a child may feel under pressure to use English at school although this is not the language in which s/he is able best to 'make individual utterances'. As Dodson points out, difficulties can arise, whatever the degree of fluency, if inappropriate languages are used or expected to be used. The question of deciding what the preferred language may be is not always easy since observation of language use alone may not provide answers which allow for the possibility that the child may feel compelled to use an 'inappropriate' language.

Schools will want to know as accurately as possible, what languages the child habitually uses at home and what the levels of literacy of parents and children may be. Wherever possible, then, it is helpful to be specific in identifying the language or languages used. However, as a general term, first language will be used with acknowledgement of its inaccuracy.

Chapter 2

Learning Language

Children come to school as fluent, although not yet fully developed, users of at least one language. How that language is supported and developed is crucial for their educational success. But most of their learning, at least in the school situation, will take place in English and English will be important for their success and achievement in British society. Teachers' attitudes to and understanding of the language acquisition process will affect the provision that they make for language development in the classroom and the curriculum.

Language development

There is little disagreement that the process of learning a first language is a complex and significant one, but there are differences of opinion about how that process takes place.

It is generally accepted that children acquire their first language with little or no direct tuition, mainly from the adults and older children around them. It is rarely the case that children's grammatical mistakes are corrected, at least in the early stages, although later parents or other adults may attempt to alter what they perceive as 'bad' or 'incorrect' language, poor pronunciation or inappropriate terminology. Adults typically respond to what children say, not how they say it.

Studies of interactions between adults and young children suggest that the adults adapt their language to the child, using language that they deem children will be able to understand and providing all sorts of supportive and confirming strategies to do so. They use tone of voice, gesture and facial expression to reinforce understanding while engaged in a range of activities. Conversations develop that are based on children's interest in the here-and-now and are frequently initiated by the child. These dialogues often involve natural repetition, but imitation by the child appears to make up a very small proportion of their utterances. Instead what appears to be happening is that the child is developing a set of rules, the grammar of the language, which gradually approximate more closely to the adult grammar.

Children, for example, learn standard ways of making plurals in English by adding an 's'. Having at an earlier stage used irregular plurals quite correctly they then seem to go through a stage where they overgeneralise a newly formulated rule and add an 's' to every plural noun. So words such as 'mouses' and 'footsies' enter their vocabulary, although the child is unlikely to have heard them in use. Eventually the irregular plural is also learnt, as an exception to a rule. The transition, therefore, to adult grammar is part of the creative, developmental process.

Chomsky suggested that since this process appears to be innate in all humans it indicated the existence of a Language Acquisition Device. It is this neuro-sensory part of the brain which enables learners to organise the disparate sounds that they hear into the systems which we know as language. Individuals not only possess a general ability to learn language, they can also develop grammars of particular languages. Chomsky put forward the concept of generative grammar, based on notions of 'deep' and 'surface' structures. Even though apparently identical utterances can have different meanings – are ambiguous – and there are often many different ways of conveying the same idea – paraphrase – we can still arrive at the deeper meanings. 'They are eating apples' can mean that those apples are suitable for eating, or that the people over there are munching apples. At a surface level the sentences are identical, yet there is a deeper understanding that leads us to the differences in meaning. Graddol et al (1994) give the example 'The chicken is ready to eat' whose deep structure depends on whether the chicken is the subject of the verb 'to eat' and is about to eat the grain, or whether it is the object and is cooked and ready to be eaten. Conversely, different surface structures, such as ' The crow dropped the cheese' or 'The cheese was dropped by the crow' can indicate identical deeper meanings.

The debate about grammars has gone on among linguists for many years. But psychologists have been more interested in observing children's use of language as part of their intellectual development. Piaget linked cognitive and linguistic development and outlined the stages through which all children move. He suggested that the understanding they have of their language environment depends on their developmental stage and that each stage is dependent on the previous one. So in the sensori-motor period in the early months of infancy, children are very limited in their physical control and need to develop these before more sophisticated skills are possible. Later concrete operations are learnt, such as concepts of conservation and inclusion. This is followed by the adult, formal operational period. Psychologists have different interpretations of the stages and argue about, for example, the ego-centric phase and the extent to which young children can decentre (see Donaldson, 1978). All this is of relevance to linguistic development because meaningful dialogue depends on shared understanding and therefore, the developing ability to see the other person's point of view.

Piaget suggested that learning, the means by which we make sense of the world, is a constructive process. He saw language as part of this, but was not particularly interested in the development of language as such. Action, he argued, was central to learning. The implications for education, taken up significantly in the Plowden Report (Central Advisory Council for Education, 1967), were that curriculum planning needed to be activity-led and based on children's capabilities at any particular age and stage of development.

The role of language in education is at the centre of much of the work of psychologists such as Vygotsky and Bruner and linguists such as Halliday. They agree that language and learning are creative processes and stress their interactive nature. The role of the more experienced adult in 'tracking' or 'scaffolding' learning is vital. Vygotsky described the distance between what a child can do alone and that which s/he can do with assistance as the 'Zone of Proximal Development', (Zoped) and argued that it is in this area that learning, including language learning, can best take place.

Many of the earlier psychologists and linguists had investigated language systems in laboratory situations. Halliday was interested in language as discourse. He analysed whole texts, rather than words or sentences, in their social contexts. Much of his work was seen to have very direct educational relevance and led to practical applications such as the Schools Council 'Language in Use' project and materials (Doughty et al, 1971) which made suggestions about how pupils could investigate the richness and variety of discourse for themselves. Since the mid-60s classroom studies by educationalists such as Barnes, Britton, Rosen and others have greatly added to our understanding of the links between language and learning. At the start of the debate about the National Curriculum, the Kingman Report (DES, 1988) gave rise to the Language in the National Curriculum (LINC) Project based explicitly based on Halliday's model of language.

The notion of language development itself encompasses growing proficiency in a number of skills. The first of these is grapho-phonic. Users have to be able to cope with the sounds and symbols of the vocabulary of the language sufficiently well to understand and make themselves understood. We all learn to adapt to different speech patterns, stress and intonation and we learn to decode a variety of fonts, styles and forms of handwriting. But only within margins of recognisability.

Secondly, there are the syntactic features of the language. These are the rules by which the language is constructed. Halliday pointed to the importance of the semantic skills, those which relate to meaning. The same or similar meaning can be conveyed by different vocabulary and grammatical structures. Part of the context in which meaning is transmitted is included in the socio-linguistic features of the language. This includes knowledge about conversational norms, how to adjust one's speech to the listener and take into account their contribution to the dialogue. It also includes the situation in which utterances take place, including the purpose and audience. Bruner (1986) adds the pragmatic criterion; 'how people use their language' (p.82) to the syntactic and semantic features. These areas are clearly inter-related and are all a necessary part of effective communication.

Second language acquisition

Many of the theories and debates about first language acquisition and its relation to learning are also considered by those who are interested in second, and subsequent, language learning.

Krashen's 'innate learning processors'; Affective Filter, Organiser and Monitor, operate much like Chomsky's Language Acquisition Device in that they describe ways in which language learners appear to process input. Krashen and his colleagues (Dulay, Burt and Krashen, 1982) used examples from research from many countries and different groups of learners to outline the second language acquisition process and to suggest practical implications.

The effective language environment, as they saw it, consists of natural communication being used for communicative purposes. Learners need to make meaning of the language they hear around them, so that one of the teacher's tasks must be to provide 'comprehensible input'. By this Krashen meant utterances that were supported by extra-linguistic clues to make their meaning clear. These clues could take the form of gestures, mime, pictures, practical activities, artefacts etc – in fact anything which made the meaning of the words clear to the listener or reader.

But, as psychologists agree, receptive understanding generally precedes production and Krashen suggested that for second language learners a number of internal processes were taking place to enable them to use the target language. He suggested that the Affective Filter accounted for the emotional state of the learner and their motivation to learn. Certainly for learners of English in British schools their reasons for learning English and their perceptions of what it means to be 'British' and their place in society, will affect their attitudes to the language. If British schooling and culture are perceived as replacing their existing language and backgrounds then this may well affect motivation. Whether positively or negatively will depend on how accepted they feel and wish to be, their ambitions and personal history and sense of identity.

Krashen also described the Organiser as having a very similar function to the Language Acquisition Device in that it unconsciously organises and formulates the rules of the target language. He moved nearer to Piaget in suggesting that there was a particular order in which items of English were acquired and that there was very little point in attempting to teach forms for which learners were not ready. He supported this suggestion with research from many different first language learners and, with some individual differences, provided evidence of the natural order.

For example, correct word order in simple and compound sentences, and the seemingly complicated use of pronouns, seem to be acquired early. Irregular past tenses are acquired relatively late, but even later appears to be use of the past participle 'en', as in 'They have taken the dog for a walk.'

He developed the concept of 'comprehensible input' into what he called the 'input hypothesis'. In order to provide language that is understandable, the teacher must not only have an idea of what the pupil can already understand but also of what the next item might be according to the natural order. His formula of i+1 (input plus one) suggests Chomsky's notion of the Zone of

Proximal Development, or Zoped: input that is a little beyond the learner's existing comprehension, but supported in such a way as to make it comprehensible. It is in this way, Krashen suggests, that learning can take place.

The idea of comprehensible input was embraced enthusiastically by practitioners. They often saw it in terms of providing a rich and active environment which would in itself produce language development for bilingual learners. Unfortunately comprehensible input on its own is not enough. It requires an understanding of pupil need – the appropriate input needs to be provided at the right time. The input must be relevant to the learning but since learning is an active process it must also be of interest and relevance to the pupils. As many studies have shown, what the teacher plans may be different from what s/he teaches and different again from what pupils learn. Learners are much more active in their learning than Krashen allowed and utilise all their experiences in the process.

An understanding of the creative process involved in forming the rules of a language helps us to look at error in a developmental way. 'Mistakes' that learners make can be analysed to illuminate the move between the languages. Krashen acknowledged that this occurs in second as in first language acquisition and advised teachers not to focus on errors but to expect and correct them by naturally providing accurate models of the language.

Bilingual learners have an advantage over those acquiring their first language in that they have their existing language experience to draw on. For many, particularly older learners, Krashen suggested, the Monitor plays an important part. This is the conscious aspect of language learning, which can be facilitated by vocabulary lists, grammar exercises and drills. Memory plays a big part in the Monitor and, provided the other aspects are in place, can help pupils to succeed. In his later work Krashen modified his ideas about the Monitor, recognising its failure to account for observed, individual differences in second language learners.

Unfortunately Krashen had very little to say about first language that was constructive. He recognised that it did not interfere with the second language and that code-switching, moving naturally from one language to another during discourse, took place, but he placed little importance on the development of first language. In fact he considered learning a second language to be largely separate from learning the first and advised teachers that:

> The second language is a new and independent language system. Since successful second language learners keep their languages distinct, teachers should too. No reference need be made to the student's first language unless the student requests it. (Dulay, Burt and Krashen, p.269)

The significance of first language skills and their importance in second language acquisition in learning was acknowledged by Cummins (1984). He was interested in the nature of language proficiency and concerned that in many cases incorrect assumptions were made about the understanding that second language learners displayed. He found it helpful to put language use initially into two categories which related to the educational needs of bilingual learners. Superficial fluency he called Basic Interpersonal Communicative Skills (BICS) and more advanced skills he called Cognitive Academic Language Proficiency (CALP).

BICS was concerned with pronunciation, grammar and vocabulary and with cognitive conversational aspects such as knowledge, comprehension and application of knowledge. CALP was of a higher order and connected to the language of meaning and function and concepts of analysis, synthesis and evaluation. One of the difficulties with this categorisation was that it seemed to suggest that early language acquisition was conceptually impoverished.

Over the course of his writing he has changed his definition, accepting the criticism that the dichotomy was too crude. He later saw second language learning as a continuum and connected the level of cognitive demand with contextual support (see diagrams 1 and 2 on page 22).

The cognitive demands depend on both internal factors, such as familiarity with the concepts and motivation, and external factors such as the level of complexity and abstraction of the ideas. Cummins later (1991) refers to the learning situation simply as contextualised or decontextualised. By this he means the presence or absence of non-linguistic cues. The notion of context indicates the importance of the situation in which a new idea or language item is introduced. Donaldson (1978) uses the term 'context-embedded' to refer to a situation which is familiar or immediate and suggests that this is supportive of communication and thought.

> It is when we are dealing with people and things in the context of fairly immediate goals and intentions and familiar patterns of events that we feel most at home. And when we are asked to reason about these things, even verbally and at some remove from them, we can often do it well (p. 76).

Diagram 1: Range of Contextual Support and Degree of Cognitive Involvement in Communicative Activities

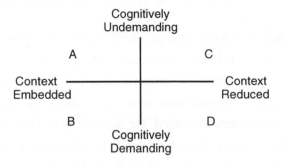

from Cummins, 1984, p.139

Diagram 2: The 'dual iceberg' Representation of Bilingual Proficiency

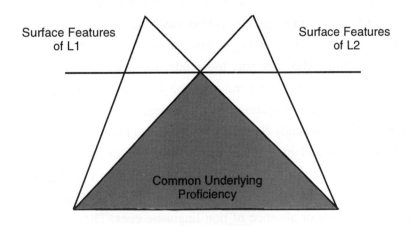

from Cummins, 1984, p.143

Cummins and Swain (1986) refer to immediate feedback and negotiation of meaning between the participants and to 'paralinguistic' and situational cues. They argue that 'Context-embedded communication derives from inter-personal involvement in a shared reality which obviates the need for explicit linguistic elaboration of the message' (p. 153).

This suggests that context-embedded situations are characterised by being face-to-face. Cummins (1984) uses Krashen's terms to discuss this form of communication, as those 'cues necessary to make the language input compre-hensible'. The cues include the learners' previous experiences, use of first language, concrete examples and paralinguistic features.

For educational purposes we may need to clarify what we mean by context. If it is merely the learning environment then the terms context-embedded or context-reduced offer little practical guidance. Edwards and Mercer (1987) refined the term context to; 'refer to everything that the participants in a conversation know and understand, over and above that which is explicit in what they say, that contributes to how they make sense of what is said ' (p. 63).

Context for them is not merely a feature of the physical and practical learning situation. It includes all the shared understanding that learners and teachers bring to the environment and that affects learning. This implies that teachers need to uncover what the learner knows and perceives and to make their own interpretations explicit. It can include understanding complex, abstract concepts as well as simple, practical ideas and applications.

In his review and critique of Cummins' model, Canale (1984) suggested that it might be more helpful to identify four components of communicative competence. These he saw as grammatical competence, sociolinguistic com-petence – covering appropriate use in different contexts, discourse competence – how language is combined in different ways to create understanding, and strategic competence. By the latter he meant both the verbal and non-verbal strategies that we use to deal with breakdowns or misunderstandings and the way in which we can enhance meaning through intonation, stress, loudness etc. These categories are similar to the grapho-phonic, syntactic, semantic and pragmatic language skills identified by linguists and discussed earlier.

Cummins specifically included first language as an important part of the second language acquisition process. He saw proficiency in either language as resting on a Common Underlying Proficiency and argued that there was strong evidence for the interdependence of language skills. If children have reached a 'threshold' fluency in their first language then many of the skills and, he

Guidelines for supporting language learning in school

Strategies that help bilingual learners will also be supportive of monolingual pupils.

- Give children opportunities to use their existing and developing language skills in real learning situations. This is where they will meet and use natural language for real purposes. They should be able to ask questions, make statements, provide explanations, express emotions – in other words, use a full range of language functions for learning.

- Provide a range of language models, peers, teachers, other adults and texts, in a range of different organisational situations, individual, small group, whole class, pairs, formal and informal. In this way all pupils receive and provide maximum exposure to language.

- Allow plenty of opportunity for bilingual learners to listen to English and respond to it before expecting them to speak. Responses can be through gesture, participation in an activity or first language. Teachers should remember and be reassured by the fact that silence does not necessarily indicate lack of thought or understanding. Active listening is an important part of learning for all of us.

- Do not correct errors but regard them as indicators of progress. Overemphasising 'correctness' can inhibit learners with the result that they may only be willing to use language with which they feel safe. If learners hear English being used naturally in a variety of circumstances they will develop an understanding of its rules and irregularities. There may be some language items for which learners at any particular stage are not yet ready.

- Expect pupils to communicate when they need to and are ready to do so. This means that opportunities for communication have to be provided and that we must respond to what the learner is trying to communicate and not to how they are doing it. Meaning is more important than form.

- Use ways other than through English to make learning comprehensible, for example real objects, pictures, practical activities, use of first language etc.

- Ensure a supportive and stress-free environment in which language and learning can take place. This will often be in a small group, and thought needs to be given to the composition of such groups. It will also include other forms of classroom organisation. Trying to operate in a language in which you are not fluent is stressful and tiring. so learners need restful times during the day.

- Peer reinforcement and social interaction are powerful factors. Children, particularly at the early stages, will probably learn more from each other than from teachers or other adults. Think and talk about how this can be best achieved. Much of it will be outside the classroom and beyond the control of the teacher. What pupils learn is both more than and different to what teachers teach.

- Support for first language will enhance, not hinder the acquisition of English. Concepts developed in L1 are transferred to L2. (Strategies for using children's first languages are discussed more fully in chapter 3.)

- Focus on supporting cognitive development in an appropriate linguistic context. This means that planning must take linguistic aspects of the learning into consideration and provide opportunities for feedback on language skills as well as learning. Natural repetition is supportive although drills and exercises are not generally helpful. Literacy skills need to be developed alongside oral language.

- Assessment should be in relation to the curriculum and not language performance. Most assessment takes place through language, but a bilingual learner's fluency in English should not be assumed to give an accurate indication of conceptual understanding. Bilingual learners should not be given Special Needs support when it is not appropriate, nor should they be denied it simply because they are bilingual. Assessment of Special Educational Need is complex and should not be undertaken too soon after the child arrives in school. Effective language learning is not dependent on intelligence.

- Approaches and resources which educate for equality and against racism will enhance pupils' learning. A relevant curriculum is one that acknowledges the lives and experiences of pupils and enables them to evaluate these experiences and control their responses. Materials need to be interesting and challenging for all students. (Chapter 5 deals more fully with these issues.)

- Build on what children bring to the learning situation. In the case of bilingual pupils this includes their first language and their knowledge and understanding of languages and how they operate.

claimed, the concepts they have acquired, are transferable to the second language.

> An immigrant child who arrives in North America.... understanding the concept of 'honesty' in his or her L1 only has to acquire a new label in L2 for an already-existing concept. (Cummins, 1984,p.144)

This prior knowledge of language systems and their operation is a significant difference between the acquisition of first and subsequent languages. Bilinguals, as accomplished users of language, already know the sorts of things that language can do in communication and when it has to be supplemented, perhaps by gesture, or altered, in tone or vocabulary. They already know about conversations and, although they may not know all the new cultural conventions, they are at least aware that conventions are likely to exist. They will have, even if they are not fully literate, some concept of symbolic representation and the differences between spoken and written language. And they will have used language in a wide variety of ways in their conceptual development. So what is suggested here is more than simple transferability. Bilingual learners, because of their intellectual and cognitive development, as well as their linguistic experiences, can have more control and direction in their second language learning.

Connected to this but adding a further dimension to the difference between first and second language acquisition is the question of age. It might appear that young learners who are still developing their linguistic skills and who are placed in an educational environment where the emphasis is on practical activities to encourage talk, interaction and literacy development, would learn English more rapidly than their older siblings. This does not, however seem to be the case. For many reasons, including self-awareness, sociability, motivation, attitude to risk-taking and existing language and learning skills, older children are more efficient language learners (see Fillmore, 1991). Younger children are, however, at an advantage in having time on their side.

If Cummins' concept of common underlying proficiency is helpful it also suggests that learners who already have a level of fluency and conceptual development in their first language will find the transfer to second language 'labels' smoother and more relevant. Collier (1989) supports this view and summarises the research evidence:

When children's L1 development is discontinued before it is completed, they may experience negative cognitive effects in L2 development; conversely, children who have reached full cognitive development in two languages enjoy cognitive advantages over monolinguals... Older children (ages 8 to 12) who have had several years of L1 schooling are the most efficient acquirers of L2 school language (p.517).

When children are learning their first language they do it in a non-threatening environment, surrounded on the whole by people who take their language development seriously and encourage them. This is an ideal situation in which to take the kind of risks that are necessary for effective learning. Second language learners are exposing themselves in what they may well see as a hostile or unsupportive environment and are often relatively isolated and vulnerable, surrounded, as they are by peers many of whom are already fluent English speakers. Particularly if their existing skills are undervalued, they may feel very insecure, embarrassed, frustrated and rejected.

Research and experience provide us, then, with evidence that many of the conditions for successful second language acquisition are the same as for the first, but that there are also crucial differences between the two.

Moving between languages

Most children have to learn to adapt their speech patterns to the requirements of schooling. They learn what vocabulary and tone to use in different situations, they learn what phrases and forms of English are acceptable, they adapt their register. They usually do all this without explicit instruction, through listening and observing and gauging the reactions of others. On occasion they may be corrected, but normally new rules are absorbed through trial and error.

Just as every teacher has their own methods of organisation and their own teaching style so they have individual expectations of behaviour and language use. By the time pupils reach secondary age they have to learn to adapt to these differing expectations every hour or so, as the timetable demands. In primary schools children have somewhat longer to learn what teachers find acceptable.

Standard English, the language of most literary texts, is also likely to be used in the classroom, although sometimes with a local accent. But a form of the local vernacular is probably the language of the playground and street. This dialect may differ quite markedly in its syntax from the standard. It may be a Creole, recognised by an increasing number of linguists as languages rather than dialects. Children learn to move between their languages or dialects. They do so more readily and easily if the status and structure of those forms of language are recognised and discussed in the classroom and not simply regarded as degraded or 'broken'. The explicit study of knowledge about language has a contribution to make to developing fluency.

At a time when linguists were conceptualising the bilingual as someone who had two or more separate and distinct languages at their disposal, it was suggested that developing bilinguals sometimes confused the two. This led to contrastive analysis, a process by which errors in one language were assumed to be due to interference from the other. If teachers could identify these features, it was argued, then they could teach and practice the correct forms which were affected by the differences.

There are a number of difficulties with this approach. On a practical level it demands that effective teachers have a working knowledge of all the languages of the pupils. Research found that in fact the errors made by second language learners did not seem to reflect the structures of their first languages and indeed many predicted errors did not occur. Talking to bilinguals about their language development indicates that they make judgements about their use of second language on the basis of their existing knowledge of that language, not because of the structures in their first language.

A theory of 'interlanguage', rather than interference, was developed to explain language shift. Learners, it was suggested, construct rules which gradually approximate to the target language, based on their developing exposure to and use of that language, in ways very similar to those used in the acquisition of first languages. This theory emphasises the importance of errors as signs of development. It sees the learner as an active builder on existing skills and knowledge, and the two languages as evidence of increasing language proficiency, as in Cummins' model of common underlying proficiency.

An analysis of linguistic errors seems to indicate that most are developmental in nature and not interlingual. This suggests that in terms of teaching, drills and exercises will be less effective than sensitive feedback, models of correct language use and discussion about language.

Evidence of code-switching confirms the interdependence of languages as opposed to the separatist, interference view. Rather than making a conscious translation bilinguals move naturally and often unconsciously between languages. They do not make mistakes and they do not confuse the languages they are using. They change because of their views of appropriacy, connected with the subject matter, the cultural context and the audience.

There seem to be three main types of code-switching. Tags – the question phrases such as 'isn't it', 'don't you' – are often in a different language from the rest of the sentence. Secondly, whole phrases or even sentences are sometimes replaced. Thirdly, individual words or phrases seem to be exchanged or borrowed. In this case the word endings, or inflections, take on the form of the language of the sentence. Examples of vocabulary borrowing proliferate in English, where we incorporate words such as 'bungalow', 'alcohol' and 'igloo' as if they were genuinely English in origin, using the grammar of English rather than that of the languages from which they derive.

Practical implications – classroom practice

Teachers always have to match their planning and organisation to the needs of the learners. They expect pupils' needs to be somewhat varied and are practised in differentiation, by input and outcome, to cater for this. They are skilled in using various methods of formal and informal assessment to judge a pupil's abilities. And they are guided by the National Curriculum both in what to teach, and what the child can be expected to have been taught.

The presence of bilingual learners, whether new arrivals or long-standing members of the school community, may make these matters both more urgent and more difficult. We need to assess what pupils are capable of in order to provide adequate support. This is a continuous process which involves observation as well as responding to children's work. However, we also need to be aware that any assessment is susceptible to bias. If a pupil is not able to perform as expected there could be a number of reasons. The concepts might be in place but the language still be inadequate to express them. Learning might have been impeded by lack of understanding of the task or the explanation. A learner may not yet have the cognitive background to develop the new understanding, or have experiences and learning styles that lead him/her to approach it in a different way. So matching learning to need is a flexible and developing process.

Many different schemes and frameworks have been suggested and tried (see, for example, Widdowson, 1979 Mohan, 1986 or Cline and Frederickson, 1991). Their main advantage is that each in its own way seeks to systematise the planning. There are, unfortunately, no textbooks or packs that will do the job for us. We need to analyse the learning and language demands of the classroom and the activities we plan in order to organise and adapt them for our students.

Any planning involves consideration of the cognitive, linguistic and social-organisational aspects of teaching and learning. Most of us do this implicitly and automatically. It may help if these considerations become more explicit. One way in which this can happen is if we are working with specialists on a team-teaching or collaborative basis. But all too often we plan for classes on our own, and often in a hurry. Nevertheless, we need to be clear about what we are teaching and why and what demands the learning presents.

a) Cognitive demands

We need to be aware of the knowledge, concepts and skills we want our pupils to develop. Many will relate directly to National Curriculum programmes of study, but usually we will subdivide and extend the outlines given in the documents. We will certainly have ideas about how they can be most effectively taught.

When teaching about the differences between the properties of metals and non-metals for example we may want pupils to understand about conduction of heat and electricity and also to relate this knowledge to its practical applications and implications and to think about whether there are any exceptions to the general rules they discover. Part of the process will involve skills of description, classification and generalisation. There are also the practical and safety aspects of experimentation. Not all these will necessarily be covered during one lesson. We often plan for a series of connected lessons or sessions.

An example from primary English might be more obviously related to language. Picture books, as well as being very important in the reading development of young children, can also be used with older children to encourage them think about the relationship between pictures and text and to explore different viewpoints and aspects of narrative. The cognitive demands might involve concepts of narrative and sequencing, understanding the differences between pictures and writing and the ability to put themselves into the role of others. Skills might include the ability to plan their own contribution and to understand and appreciate the views of their peers (see Baddeley and Eddershaw, 1994 and Graham, 1996).

The extent to which these objectives are cognitively demanding will largely depend on the experiences of the learners. Teachers may have fairly accurate ideas about the learning of pupils who have had all their schooling in

Britain and whose backgrounds they know and possibly share, but for many bilingual pupils such assumptions cannot be made.

In order to make it as likely as possible that the concepts will be accessible we will need to choose resources that reflect the backgrounds of the pupils concerned. In the science example this may involve metal artefacts from various cultures; perhaps cooking utensils from India or musical instruments from Nigeria. We must be careful when we select resources that we are not being patronising or inadvertently reinforcing images of 'backwardness'. If real items cannot be obtained pictures are a reasonable alternative.

Before exploring picture books we may wish to reinforce some of the skills by using a set of familiar pictures to sequence and discuss. We will also need to explain the task carefully so that pupils realise the point of working with a story that is intended for younger children.

There are many other strategies we can use to support understanding. Practical activities themselves are a non-linguistic way to learn. But as we participate in activities, whether model making, experiments, cooking or role-play, we must try to make the learning aims clear to the pupils. Traditionally teachers have done this by initially explaining the tasks and then clarifying further in response to children's questions. This is often followed by teachers asking questions in order to check pupils' understanding. But there are other ways to help children reflect on their learning. They should be encouraged to design activities which solve problems based on their own questions. This need not demand very complex language. For example, the science inquiry could begin with a number of items, real or pictures, which pairs of pupils could be asked to 'sort into two piles' according to their own criteria. They could then list and name the groups, being helped with a chart and labels if necessary. Lists could then be shared with another group, together with the criteria for their classification. Any discrepancies would be discussed and pupils should be encouraged to ask questions about what else they want to find out. Although early stage learners might not be fully involved in all the discussions, the use of real objects or pictures and a chart to systematise the learning would make the cognitive aspects more accessible to them.

To summarise what they have discovered, pupils can be given a set of statements from which to select the one that most nearly matches their learning, or to sort into piles of 'true' or 'false'. It is often easier to agree or disagree with given sentences than to compose one's own.

Learning tasks need to be 'unpacked' to help pupils understand them. We sometimes provide too much information at one time rather than giving pupils time to orientate themselves and anticipate their learning. Learning aims should be shared with the learners.

In preparation for a new text, for example, pictures or even video material can help to set the scene. A diagram or summary of the plot, or a series of headings or questions which we are hoping to have answered by the text, can be helpful. Another strategy is to ask pupils to anticipate the events. We do this for ourselves when we choose our own reading, often by consulting a review or the 'blurb', or flicking through the book for an indication of content and style. To make some of the expectations and conventions explicit can be a way of preparing the reader.

One strategy that is sometimes suggested to make learning more accessible is to simplify the tasks or language. Often, however, extension and amplification rather than simplification are the best strategy. Redundancy in language and in activities can be helpful in providing additional information in another and perhaps more suitable way. By simplifying and removing what we see as unnecessary we may well be reducing rather than improving clues to understanding. Equally, tasks themselves can be designed to involve repetition which reinforces learning and language. Extra input in the form of examples and explanation before, during and after an activity can help to clarify concepts.

Another way of reinforcing understanding through repetition is by going back over work. This can be done by one group of pupils in order to inform another group who have done something slightly different. The learner can be reminded about what has already been done through a series of statements or pictures which could be sequenced to replicate the activity. A paragraph could be re-organised or written from scratch, in either L1 or L2, or summarised in single words or headings. Diagrammatic representations are very helpful ways of showing the underlying organisation of concepts. Concept maps of the learning can be made by pupils (see Johnson, 1992, Novak and Gowin, 1984) Mohan's work on knowledge frameworks which links the theoretical and practical skills needed to make concepts accessible, can be adapted to provide a similar approach (see Mohan, 1986).

b) Social demands

Any learning situation places social and organisational demands on the learners. Pupils will work on their own, with the teacher or other adult acting as guide and at other times the teaching will be to the whole class. The benefits of small group learning and of collaboration are increasingly recognised. But each of these learning situations places different demands on the learners.

Reid *et al* (1989) suggest a five stage model of learning. The first stage is engagement. CLIS (Children Learning in Science Project) call this the orientation phase. It is an introduction to the subsequent learning and provides an opportunity for sharing understanding and expectations. This, they suggest, is the stage which is most frequently taught to the whole class and when new content is introduced. It is therefore vital that pupils really do 'engage'.

Whole class learning has the benefit for bilinguals that they are not singled out but may be able to listen and rehearse ideas privately. To do this, however, they must be able to see and hear everything that is going on. Any material or text that the teacher refers to must be clearly visible. It is also beneficial for bilingual learners to be able to see the speaker so that they can pick up para-linguistic clues such as gesture or facial expression. The pupils will need a clear understanding of what help they can expect from the teacher and how to ask for it. Asking questions or speaking up in a large group is always difficult and more so for someone who is not confident in English.

The pressures of working on an individual basis, with or without a teacher, are different again and depend very much on the relationships which have been established. To be the focus of attention for any length of time can be stressful, but so can the isolation of working alone. Such situations are a normal part of most classrooms, but they can place considerable demands on bilingual pupils.

Small group, collaborative work is often the most successful learning situation for all pupils. It allows them to test and question what they already know and to experiment with new ideas. They can learn from each other as well as from the material provided by the teacher. But productive collaboration does not automatically occur simply by putting pupils in small groups. The task and materials have to be carefully planned so that each member of the group can be an active learner. The teacher's role is as planner, facilitator and evaluator, rather than as transmitter of information. An important aspect of the planning will result from monitoring social interaction.

Many primary and some secondary classrooms are organised on a co-operative basis. Pupils sit in pairs or small groups around a table and work on the same task. They sometimes talk about what they are doing and help each other, for example by giving spellings, sharing equipment or answering individual queries. This in itself is not collaborative learning, although it may be a precursor and pre-requisite of collaboration. Collaborative learning is not the same as group work, although it is often most successful when organised this way. If we believe that learning is a social, interactive and constructive process then we need to plan for it to be so, and this is often through active collaboration.

Friendship groups are sometimes the best way of arranging collaboration, but there are times when differently organisationed groups may be advantageous. Children may learn more from someone whose views they do not share than from a friend with whom they often talk. Whether to organise pupils in single-sex or mixed groups will depend on the purpose of the activity. Bilingual pupils could at times be in groups which share a common language and would at other times benefit from working with monolingual English speakers. Learners should get used to changing and mixing groups. Pairs are often a good way to start. They can then combine to form fours or sixes. Alternatively, seven or eight pupils can sub-divide into pairs or threes for particular tasks and then feedback on their work to the larger group.

It is important in planning to make the purpose of the work clear, both to ourselves and to our pupils. Edwards and Mercer (1987) argue that lack of explicit intention on the part of the teacher marks the beginning of a communicative breakdown that leads to ritualised learning. Too rarely do we share with pupils the reasons for doing a particular activity or what the learning outcomes might be. If children have the opportunity to discuss and clarify learning objectives – and often small groups are the least threatening context for doing this – they can then begin to understand and share the teacher's intentions.

The organisation of the activity and its outcomes also need to be planned, bearing in mind the support that pupils will require from the materials, each other and staff. All learners need to be able to make a contribution to the joint enterprise and this will involve talk. Collaborative learning is based on the premise that pupils bring a great deal of knowledge to the situation and that they can learn from each other as well as from other sources. We often understand and sort out our own ideas and arguments most clearly when we have to explain them to others.

Teachers will also need to decide on their own role during an activity. Small group work provides an excellent opportunity for observation, but at other times teachers need to be facilitators, providers of information and injectors of ideas, regulators and controllers and to judge when to intervene and when to stand back from a situation.

Collaboration takes place on many levels. It can involve pairs of pupils sharing a book or being writing consultants. Science experiments are frequently co-operative and, if they take the form of problem-solving, are often collaborative too. Sturman (1988) describes how collaborative work with Yr 3 involved pairs and larger groups, with and without adult involvement, in writing letters, making posters and tape-recordings and eventually making contact with a school in Nicaragua. By working in this way the children became agents for change, tackling issues collectively that would have been impossible on an individual basis.

When using collaborative methods teachers relinquish some control to the pupils, encouraging and enabling them to take greater responsibility for their own learning and respecting their knowledge. Education for equality implies a classroom that is open and in which ideas and information are exchanged and respected, where positive criticism and evaluation are encouraged and issues of racism, bias, omission and stereotyping are discussed and challenged.

The social demands of learning can be made more manageable if they are carefully planned. Seating arrangements, how teachers use their voice, visual presentation and clarity of instruction will all help to make pupils feel more at ease. We need to be aware of the hidden curriculum which determines some of the classroom rules and to make it explicit and consistent when necessary. Children are well able to organise themselves if they know where to put books and equipment, what they always need to have with them, and how the teacher deals with lateness, requests for the toilet, setting and collecting in homework.

Much group work will entail talk and movement. The rules governing both should be discussed and agreed and the furniture organised to minimise noise and facilitate movement. All learners have their preferred style and for some of the bilinguals, particularly if they have been educated in a different tradition, group work may seem strange at first. Patience and careful explanation are essential . Research and the experience of pupils and teachers confirm that collaborative learning is of real and lasting benefit to all, and particularly to bilingual learners. Collaborative learning needs to be carefully planned and prepared and teachers, who may have reservations about its usefulness, need the confidence to implement genuine group work, in a small way initially, and evaluate its effectiveness.

c) Language demands

Almost all learning involves language – written or spoken. For bilingual learners, particularly those at an early stage of developing English, it is the language of the classroom that will be most demanding. If teachers are aware of the nature of some of these demands they can go a long way to meeting their pupils' needs.

All languages differ in the way their vocabulary and structures convey meaning. English nouns have no gender, whereas many other languages attach gender, including neuter in some cases, to nouns and to the adjectives that agree with them. In English the pronoun 'you' can be singular or plural, so that a sentence such as 'He will give it to you' gives no indication of what 'it' might be, nor of how many 'you' refers to.

In many other languages pronouns differentiate not only between singular and plural, as do most in English, but also indicate the degree of formality being used. English, unlike many languages, uses both a definite and in-definite article – 'the' and 'a'. English also has a typical word order, subject, verb, object, :He ate the orange. whereas other languages might, for example indicate meaning by the addition of suffixes or prefixes indicating tense, case or plurality.

Fluent speakers of any language have an understanding of structure and meaning so that if they do not hear a complete sentence they can make an enlightened guess about parts they have missed. We know which words are likely to go together, which are synonyms, antonyms and so on. We automatically employ 'collocation' – the way in which particular words work together. In English for example 'we face problems and *interpret* dreams, but in modern Hebrew we have to *stand in front* of problems and *solve* dreams' (Crystal p.105). This is part of the process of learning any language and each one has its own cultural associations. We may all have somewhat different images of what is involved in 'preparing tea' or 'making a cup of tea'.

Spoken language has a particular rhythm and intonation which conveys meaning. The tone and stress that is placed on a word or sentence may be unfamiliar to speakers of other languages. We can use the same words to ask a question or make a statement, depending on intonation. Similarly, an apology can take several syntactic forms such as: 'I am sorry', ' I won't do that again', 'I didn't see it' or 'My mistake.'

To help our pupils to cope with such language demands we cannot and do not need to know all their languages. Nor should we speak unnaturally loudly or slowly. We need to be aware, however, that understanding meaning is not simply a matter of receiving language. Communication is an interactive process that involves interpretation on the part of the listener as well as production by the speaker. As much information as possible, therefore, needs also to be conveyed by means other than language. Statements can be phrased in several ways and reinforced by gesture, mime, demonstration and example. Some hearers will find a written repetition useful. Interpretation into first language will also be helpful but is not always possible. Above all we need to be sensitive to the possibility of misunderstanding and to listen attentively to the responses and questions of our pupils.

It is clear that spoken language is interactive. Literacy also involves active engagement with the written word. We are not simply passive receivers of a printed message, we bring our own knowledge of print and literary and cultural conventions to everything we read or write. Most European languages use a Roman script that is written from left to right and sits on the line. Some have extra letters or different diacritical marks, such as accents. Greek and Russian are among those that use different scripts but they have straight-forward letter-sound relationships. Other languages may be quite different, being read from right to left, like Urdu and Arabic for example, or from top to bottom, like Chinese. Some use symbols for syllables or represent vowels differently from consonants. Others use characters to represent an idea rather than a sound. Some differentiate upper and lower case, whereas others only have one form of script. Punctuation conventions also vary.

Reading or copying an unfamiliar script, particularly if it is handwritten, is a painstaking task. It is not always easy to decide what is material to the symbol and what is an embellishment or idiosyncrasy. This becomes even more difficult if the original is at some distance from the writer, for example on a blackboard or OHP. It will take extra them time and accuracy may also suffer. This could in turn affect other work such as revising or redrafting from notes.

Helping children to understand written texts on many different levels is best done by looking first at the whole text and its shape and gist, and then concentrating on smaller units such as sentence and word. Fiction and non-fiction texts differ substantially in their organisation and presentation. Non-fiction generally has headings and sub-headings which provide clues to its organisation. Fiction relies more often on a straightforward narrative, which may or may not be chronological. A non-fiction text may be supported by photographs, pictures, maps and diagrams and the pictures usually have a different relationship to the text than those in a story book.

The nature of the discourse style is also different in the two types of text. Non-fiction typically uses a more impersonal style, often with fewer pronouns and using the passive tense. The sentences are often long and complex, with more clauses and a greater variety of connectives. Word patterns and sentence structures which are unfamiliar or seldom found in normal speech are more frequent in non-fiction. These are often used for effect or variety. The absence of intonation cues may obscure meaning further.

Technical or formal vocabulary is often explained in a glossary or in the text, but if a familiar word is used in an unfamiliar or specialist manner it can create confusion. A history book describing Romans in Britain discusses 'natural springs' with the assumption that readers will know that this refers to a water source rather than a season, a leap or the spiral part of a bed. The more aware we are of the misunderstandings that such aspects of text can create, the more likely we are to tackle the problems or prevent them from arising.

Strategies for support

There are many different strategies for supporting the language development of bilingual learners in the classroom. Many will already be familiar and part of teaching practice. The importance lies in the choice of appropriate strategies and this must depend on the demands of the learning and the needs of the pupils. The link between planning and evaluation and assessment is therefore crucial.

Teachers need to do more than simply provide comprehensible input. We need to give bilingual learners the skills to structure and organise their learning in a way that will develop their English as well. This means providing advice, help and guidance on starting off, by, for example *providing initial words or sentences*, or *showing pupils how to take notes and organise paragraphs*. We need to offer *explanations and examples of rules about spelling, constructing questions, forming the past tense*. We need to give *feedback in a constructive way* so that pupils can use their errors as a learning tool. All this can be started at an early age but it becomes increasingly important for older pupils who have the linguistic experience to build on and for whom time in school is limited.

The strategies can be usefully considered in relation to the *receptive* and *productive* language required. The question to ask regarding receptive language is: what English will the pupil need to understand and how can understanding be ensured? To appreciate the demands of productive language, teachers should undertake at least part of the task themselves.

Active and interactive listening can be supported by *discussion beforehand about expectations*. Discussion can include what sort of questions pupils would expect or want answers to. In the case of a story, conventions and styles can be indicated through a discussion about what might happen next. *Prediction* and *problem-solving* in, for example, science can be used to involve learners in the design of experiments and the organisation of equipment.

Well focused questions will guide listeners to what to look out for. It is often helpful if the questions are discussed in advance and repeated during or after the activity. For example when listening to a poem, children can be asked to remember all the words which indicate feelings, colour or mood. Several readings will be needed to increase familiarity and also to ensure that there is an appreciation of the whole poem as well as the focused aspect.

It is useful to *organise listening activities* in pairs or groups who share what they have retained or learned. When watching a television broadcast each member of the group can be asked to concentrate on different information. An account of, say, a shopping expedition can be broken down into 'where we went' and 'what we bought'.

Retention or classification of information can be reinforced by the use of *charts*. A class listening to an account of the solar system can be asked to tick columns or insert words when they hear the names of stars, planets or other bodies. *Pictures can be sequenced* in advance of hearing an account of a historical event and then reorganised in the light of further information.

Understanding can be reinforced by *videos, photographs, pictures, real objects or replicas and models. Trips and visits*, even if very local, are also invaluable in reinforcing understanding. Photographs taken during an outing which include the pupils themselves increase interest and can be used in many ways afterwards. One class took a short trip around the immediate locality to focus on signs and took photographs which pupils then selected, labelled and organised to make a display. Even pupils at the very early stages of learning English can be involved in taking photographs, making the selections and copying labels.

Local *museums* are often rich sources of educational material. Speculation in advance of a visit about what they might find out about the area and its history can focus the pupils' interest and attention.

The use of a *tape recorder* also provides opportunities for learners to listen again to a dialogue, story or account at their own pace and in their own time. *Story tapes* in several languages are available commercially, or children and parents can produce their own. Secondary pupils may also find it helpful if the teacher can record certain crucial parts of a lesson in advance – an outline of a plot or characters in a class novel say, or instructions about the use of a particular piece of equipment or explanation of a complicated mechanism.

The knowledge that bilinguals have about languages invites *discussion about language*: how to say things in different ways, why English uses certain constructions and how other languages express particular ideas. We must not feel that we always need be the experts, but should be willing to pool our knowledge to explore similarities and differences in language use systematically.

Many listening activities also involve talk and opportunities should be provided for bilinguals to take active part. *Role play or puppetry* are both very liberating, allowing children to take on another persona. The activity can be preceded by practice in order to increase pupils' confidence. Bilingual learners should be encouraged to take as much or as little part as they wish in the early stages, and to use their first language if preferred. *Drama activities* in which teacher and pupils step in and out of role are excellent ways of using first language for real purposes.

Interviews also provide excellent opportunities for purposeful talk. Oral history is increasingly being explored as one way of making concepts real. Preparation and rehearsal of interview skills can provide useful practice and, again, first languages can be used as appropriate. A group of children on a local environment project interviewed shop-keepers about their goods. Since some of the shops were run by bilingual members of the community the use of first language had an important function. Bilingual pupils then translated the interviews for their classmates.

Tape-recorders can be used to make a more *permanent record of talk*. It also provides an opportunity for children to make changes and corrections. A tape made for one purpose can be used again for another. For example learners talking about their reasons for matching pictures of houses to particular countries and climates can revisit the tape to discuss their roles in the activity or the different terms that they used to describe the buildings.

Games can have a useful educational purpose and do not have to be confined to the early years. They are interactive and require co-operation, particularly if the competitive element is reduced. A domino-type game involving matching symbols for electronic equipment to the appropriate label is an enjoyable way of reinforcing learning. History and geography lend themselves to different types of board games, such as snakes and ladders to indicate the changes in political fortunes of a government at a particular time, or mapping games to decide on the location of different parts of a settlement. Bilingual learners can participate in the activity, learn concepts and develop English skills while doing so. The mathematical and design-technology skills involved when pupils design and make their own games are also very valuable and can involve considerable language development in the collaborative planning.

Much of the support and reinforcement for language development in speaking and listening is best achieved in small groups where bilingual learners will take risks and test out ideas. They need to feel that they have a role and that their contributions are taken seriously. Similarly, for reading and writing the small group context can be reassuring and talk will enhance the process.

Reading is regarded as a receptive skill although understanding involves the reader in active engagement with the text. Lunzer and Gardner (1984) developed a series of strategies for accessing text known as DARTs (Directed Activities Related to Texts). These have been widely used, particularly by secondary English teachers, but also by many others who were probably not aware of the label. Essentially the techniques involve various ways of interrogating texts in order to make them meaningful. They distinguish analytical activities, which examine the main features of the writing, from reconstruction, which is a way of putting together a 'mutilated' passage in order to highlight aspects such as cohesion and continuity. Lunzer and Gardner emphasise the importance of discussion in small groups in these activities.

In approaching a new, unfamiliar text it can be helpful to focus on key aspects, such as headings, pictures and diagrams, in order first to *predict* content. Learners can then go on to *underline key words* or concepts. Using different colours for different categories can help them find their way around. If the passage itself cannot be marked then an alternative is to *label parts and fill in a table*. A text about life in another country, for example, might include information on the population, transport, agriculture and industry. Each of these could form a separate heading on a table and key words from the text, or line references, be inserted.

Alternatively, pupils could be asked to *select a title* for each paragraph or section of the text. They could either choose from a list of titles or be asked to suggest their own. A more extended version of this activity is to write or select a sentence which summarises the paragraph. Sentences which are carefully written can highlight various aspects of linguistic complexity that might need to be explained. For example, making a choice between the sentences about a text after having read the original might indicate to pupils that they need to look at a document more carefully, or to the teacher that particular concepts or language needed further attention –

If pupils' reading skills are less advanced pictures or diagrams can provide an alternative way of *labelling or summarising* a text. A description of an experiment or an industrial process can be drawn in a series of diagrams and pupils can select the correct one. Alternatively learners can make their own representations.

Understanding can be developed through *exemplification*. Case studies are an excellent method of making a depersonalised text come alive. If a description of the way of life in Victorian cities is illuminated by a series of vignettes readers can match them with the historical account. This sort of activity can also lead to *role play and improvisation* which further illustrates and reinforces meaning. Or the examples in the text can be *re-organised* and *classified.* Case studies might include examples of servants, labourers, unemployed people, traders, craftspeople and householders which could be reclassified according to whether they had the vote before certain legislation was passed or whether they became enfranchised as a result. Lists could be made about the similarities and differences in the lives of the people. Pupils could go on to discuss whether certain statements about them were 'true' or 'false' or – a useful third category – 'not enough evidence' or 'don't know'.

When planning *charts and tables* it is important to think about the uses to which they will be put. The headings and organisation can lend themselves to writing tasks. For example, infants learning about different types of bags did a number of practical activities such as matching appropriate items and their labels to each bag. Tea cartons and plastic fruit went in the shopping bag, lipstick and a comb in the make-up bag, a book and pencil-case in the school bag. The chart for the pictorial or written record, using the same labels, was headed :'———— and ———— go in / the ———— bag' so that the resulting record could be used to write sentences. Other language was introduced to show that the rubbish bag could also be called a bin liner or school bag replaced by brief-case.

Knowledge about language can be developed by re-arranging charts and headings. So, in the example above, 'The _____ bag/ is used for _____ ' would change an active into a passive sentence.

Another way of analysing text which can help learners to understand its meaning and construction is to *trace the cohesive links*. The use of pronouns and other ties often make it difficult for bilingual learners to understand the structure of a passage. Some of these refer to nouns which have already occurred, such as 'When I arrived in England it (i.e. my arrival) was a cultural shock to me'. Others indicate items that will come later in the sentence, for example 'It's broad cockney, my accent.' Link words such as 'however', 'but' and 'and' can give clues to the relationship of two clauses or sentences. So if pupils mark these textual features it can aid their understanding.

Deletion, or *cloze*, is a reconstructive way of looking closely at the use of words. Words can be deleted according to any rule, for example every seventh or eleventh word or all the colour adjectives, depending on the purpose. Leaving the 'correct' number of spaces for the letters of the missing word or having a list of replacements may be regarded as helpful although it is often unnecessarily confining and gives the impression that there is always only one answer. This sort of activity is best done in pairs or groups in which open-ended discussion about the use of a particular word can result in extremely detailed and sophisticated language. A series of words deleted from a poem can lead to highly productive discussions about why one word is 'better' than another and what it actually conveys.

Poems can be used in other ways too which help focus on language use. *Resequencing a poem* requires the learners to concentrate on all the aspects which shape the text, including flow of ideas, rhyme and rhythm, imagery and metaphor. It should be emphasised that the poet wrote a specific text but that other versions might be equally valid. It is then up to pupils to negotiate and justify their versions.

Some texts, such as poems, lend themselves to being *read aloud* and the chance for bilingual learners to hear as well as see text is important. It should not be assumed that because bilingual learners may still be developing their literacy skills they need to have shortened or simplified texts. They need more rather than fewer examples, but these need to be supported to facilitate comprehension. Every opportunity for linking the four language skills should be used to reinforce understanding.

Pictures and texts can be sequenced and matched in many ways that are supportive of understanding. At an early age children can learn to read images by being offered several captions and deciding how each affects the picture. Different pairs of pictures can be chosen to combine and a narrative developed from them. Alternative arrangements and orders lead to different stories. Sentences or longer passages can be similarly divided and re-arranged. Or a sentence can be started for pupils to complete in their own way.

After a *cooking* activity one group from Y2 invited the rest of the class to taste their dish and then explained how it was made. Having had the practical experience they all contributed orally but a set of pictures, that they had drawn immediately after doing the cooking, helped them to remember the correct sequence without omitting a vital stage and to organise themselves so that everyone in the group made a contribution. With the teacher acting as scribe, they went on to compose sentences for each picture which they matched up to complete their own record. A further development was to alter the account to add to the class recipe book. This entailed changing the tense from past to present and the pronouns from 'we' to 'you' and using suitable vocabulary to indicate sequence, such as 'first', 'then' and 'after that'. So that 'we washed the rice' became 'first you wash the rice'. Drawing attention to linguistic changes helps to make them clear for bilingual learners.

Planning for this kind of session involves anticipating some of the language demands that will be made and devising activities to support them. By encouraging learners to control, discuss, rearrange and become familiar with texts we enable them to use their existing skills and to experiment with new ones.

An important support for writing is to provide *models and examples*. As learners encounter a greater variety of texts they will become aware of some of the differences between them in terms of structure, purpose, style and typical language (see Tonjes, 1986). But without providing examples and making these differences explicit we cannot expect learners to understand them or produce them themselves. Many features are cross cultural, for instance newspapers from many countries and in different scripts can show similarities in layout and design and introduce specialist vocabulary such as 'column', 'headline', 'byline', 'caption' etc. Giving pupils the language with which to discuss their reading and writing will help them to reflect on their learning.

Part of the process of writing *involves drafting and re-drafting*. This is something which all writer do but it has to be learnt and practised if it is to become a useful skill. Bilingual learners in particular will find this process helpful to their confidence and fluency. Word-processors make the re-drafting process very simple (although lack of key-board skills can slow it down considerably) but the same principles can be applied to handwritten work. Re-drafting is not just a matter of correcting spelling mistakes and writing the passage neatly. Pupils need to be taught to look for the clarity and extension of ideas, the structure and flow of the text and the apt choice of words or phrases. Techniques of re-drafting such as using omission marks, arrows, brackets and asterisks, need to be explained.

Planning a piece of writing, often involving talk and sometimes note-taking, can also utilise some of the activities discussed above such as *re-organising or ranking statements or drawing a plan or concept map.*

The freedom with which pupils will approach a writing task depends to some extent on the response they receive from teachers. If emphasis is placed on presentation and correct spelling at an early stage then fluency and ideas may be inhibited in favour of security and brevity. Bilingual learners can be encouraged to write in their first language, with translation to follow if possible. They should have word-lists and dictionaries available and requests for help with spelling should be freely given. English spelling is difficult but governed by rules which are related to the meanings and origins, not the sounds of the words. The reasons for a word to be spelled in a particular way should be explained.

Collaborative writing enables ideas and their organisation to be discussed by pupils and worked out together. Those who are only beginning to develop literacy skills will need a partner to act as a scribe. On occasion the collaborator could be the teacher or other adult. We need to make the writing process clear to learners through demonstration and explanation. By being closely involved in the learning we are better able to understand and offer guidance about the difficulties pupils encounter.

All teachers plan their teaching. The quality and implementation of those plans, so important to ensure learning, is even more crucial for bilingual learners. We may need to *resequence activities* so that practical tasks enable learners first to identify, describe and classify the content before moving on to more abstract and linguistically complex learning such as combining, comparing and evaluating. Curriculum content can be adapted to include specific linguistic objectives. For example, a topic about invaders and explorers can include role-play which provides practice in making requests or giving directions. Next, pupils might write a narrative in which invading forces issue instructions and commands. The focus must always be on learning that is challenging and interesting, supported by appropriate language.

Pupils' needs

Effective support for bilingual learners depends on matching the demands of the learning to the needs of the pupils. Evaluation, monitoring and assessment are therefore crucial and ongoing. They involve all partners in the learning – pupils, teachers, other staff and parents.

Evaluation of the process includes judgements about the teaching. Aspects of organisation, planning, resourcing and delivery must be evaluated in order to decide what contributed to learning success or failure. If a pupil does not appear to have achieved this may be due to inadequate explanation, inappropriate resources, unhelpful grouping, the learner not having the right equipment, not being able to hear or make him/herself heard, differences in interpretation of the task – or many other reasons. One way of solving these problems is to talk to the pupils themselves or ask groups to discuss their own learning successes.

If teachers make reflective talk an aspect of their classrooms and provide models, through their discussions about how a session went and what they learnt and observed, the pupils will be more likely to see the value of self-evaluation. Helping pupils to keep their own learning log also encourages reflection.

Direct questioning will not always give clear answers. There may be many reasons for pupils saying they understand when in fact they have problems. Even a 'correct' answer may not indicate understanding. We all have strategies for guessing the 'right' answer and teachers often inadvertently indicate what they would like to hear by their tone or phraseology.

We need to provide a range of opportunities for pupils to demonstrate understanding and success, and to observe and note their achievements and areas of misunderstanding or confusion. Some of the learning outcomes will be permanent and easy to sample, others will be transitory and need to be recorded at the time. Some will be part of the process rather than the product. Checklists indicating the conditions under which an observation was made, such as in the Primary Learning Record (Hester, 1993) will help us to be

AN AID TO PRIMARY CURRICULUM PLANNING

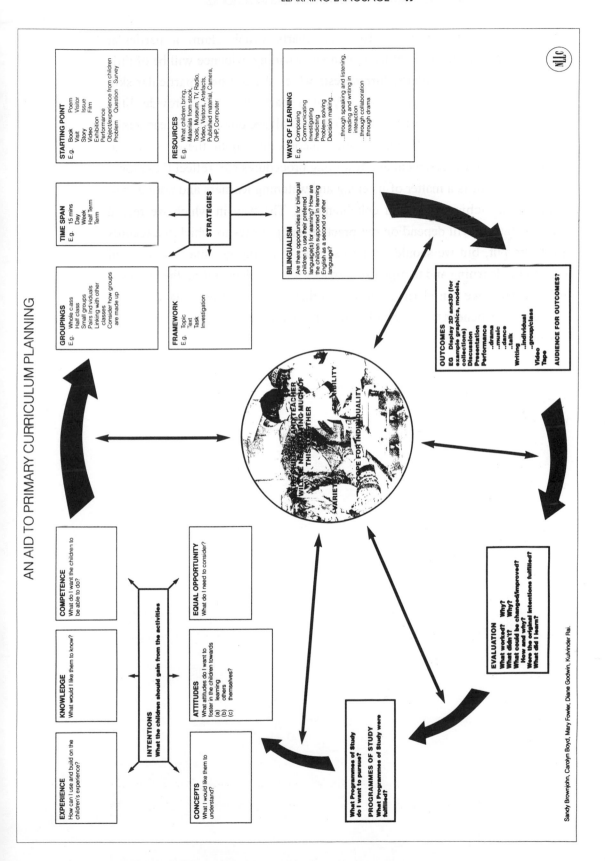

STARTING POINT
E.g. Book   Poem
     Visit   Visitor
     Story   Issue
     Video   Film
     Exhibition
     Performance
     Object/experience from children
     Problem   Question   Survey

RESOURCES
E.g. What children bring,
     Materials from stock,
     Tools, Museum, TV, Radio,
     Video, Visitors, Artefacts,
     Published material, Camera,
     OHP, Computer

WAYS OF LEARNING
E.g. Composing
     Communicating
     Investigating
     Predicting
     Problem solving
     Decision making...
     ...through speaking and listening,
        reading and writing in
        interaction
     ...through collaboration
     ...through drama

TIME SPAN
E.g. 15 mins
     Day
     Week
     Half Term
     Term

STRATEGIES

BILINGUALISM
Are there opportunities for bilingual
children to use their preferred
language(s) for learning? How are
the children supported in learning
English as a second or other
language?

GROUPINGS
E.g. Whole class
     Half class
     Small groups
     Pairs Individuals
     Linking with other
        classes
     Consider how groups
     are made up

FRAMEWORK
E.g. Topic
     Text
     Investigation

OUTCOMES
EG Display 2D and 3D (for
    example graphics, models,
    collections)
    Discussion
    Presentation
    Performance
        ...drama
        ...music
        ...dance
        ...talk
    Writing
        ...individual
        ...group/class
    Video
    Tape

AUDIENCE FOR OUTCOMES?

EXPERIENCE
How can I use and build on the
children's experience?

KNOWLEDGE
What would I like them to know?

COMPETENCE
What do I want the children to
be able to do?

INTENTIONS
What the children should gain from the activities

CONCEPTS
What I would like them to
understand?

ATTITUDES
What attitudes do I want to
foster in the children towards
(a) learning
(b) others
(c) themselves?

EQUAL OPPORTUNITY
What do I need to consider?

EVALUATION
What worked?   Why?
What didn't?   Why?
What could be changed/improved?
How and why?
Were the original intentions fulfilled?
What did I learn?

**What Programmes of Study
do I want to pursue?**

PROGRAMMES OF STUDY
**What Programmes of Study were
fulfilled?**

Sandy Brownjohn, Carolyn Boyd, Mary Fowler, Diane Godwin, Kulvinder Rai.

systematic in our provision. But tick charts which claim a particular competence on a specific occasion without providing evidence will be of little long term benefit. Similarly, formal tests which depend on a particular skill being displayed in a particular way at a particular time provide little information beyond the very specific. We must all see ourselves as teachers of content and language. If our planning incorporates both these aspects of learning then our assessment and recording procedures can reflect these too.

Assessment is a matter of listening and watching learners and noting their moments of achievement and enlightenment. The way in which we record these instances will depend on our practice and the uses to which the records are to be put, but we should get accustomed to noting genuine occasions of significant learning and to organising spaces for ourselves during the lesson or session when we can observe and record them. Taking time to stand back is ultimately of benefit to our pupils and our teaching and makes us learners in our own classrooms.

ACTIVITIES ON TEXTS

I. COMPLETE IT

These activities use a text which has been doctored so as to be incomplete in some way, with the pupils being asked to reconstruct the whole text from what they are given. There are two ways of setting this up.

i) Deleting parts of the text for pupils to replace.

The deletions might be:

(a) single words;

(b) longer sections;

(c) titles and sub-headings;

(d) parts of the text where an accompanying diagram/illustration has been left intact (or vice versa).

In any of these cases pupils can be left to decide their own replacements or, alternatively, given a choice of bits to fill the gaps (perhaps more bits than are needed or with a few rogue possibilities included).

ii) Providing parts of a text with which pupils can build a working text of their own.

Here the original text is made more radically incomplete; it might be offered for 'assembly' in these formats:

(a) cut up into sections for pupils to re-sequence;

(b) as a skeleton of headings, sub-headings and a few key statements, with pupils asked to flesh it out in some way;

(c) the complete text provided up to a given point, with the pupils then asked to hypothesise what they think might follow, given what they've read;

(d) a small key section as a 'first bite' (not necessarily from the opening of the text), with the pupils asked to read it and then speculate on what might be expected to go around it as preparation, extension, balance, etc.

2. COMPARE IT

In these activities extras are provided to go along with the text and the pupils are asked to compare and relate the text and the extras in some way.

The extra might be:

(a) simply additional texts on the same subject, with pupils asked to mark up and comment on what they see as the important similarities and differences between the version;

(b) in the form of prefabricated but as yet unassembled parts of a flow-diagram, a tabulation, a set of notes or a paraphrase which pupils are asked to put together into a version that squares with (or even extends and develops) the original (which is also given).

ACTIVITIES ON TEXTS continued

3. RE-FORM IT

In these activities pupils are encouraged to represent what they have learned from reading the text in ways which help them make it their own. All the activities here might involve pupils in underlining and labelling sections of the text in some way as a preliminary.

i) Orally, pupils could be invited to:

(a) improvise a 'talk through' of the information to a partner or small group (perhaps with support from brief notes, a flow diagram, etc.) dealing with questions both on the way through and at the end;

(b) offer a more formulated lecturette version of the above with appropriate aids or apparatus and handling a formal question time at the end;

(c) take part in a role-play simulation or sketch which draws on the ideas and information in the text.

ii) Using drawings and visuals, pupils might design:

(a) annotated doodles (ie. simple representational pictures plus cartoons);

(b) an abstract 'model' which represents the ideas in a diagrammatic form;

(c) a tabulation, chart or graph;

(d) a flow-diagram or critical-path analysis.

iii) In writing, pupils might be asked to make:

(a) linear notes (ie. traditionally organised jottings with headings, numbered sub-sections etc);

(b) patterned notes (ie. notes done as a network showing the connections between ideas);

(c) a summary (plus response), in which they give their own shortened and reorganised account of what the writer said (and what they think of it);

(d) a re-write of the information for a specified audience (possibly younger, and preferably real and available);

(e) a parody of the writer's ideas in a way that implies a comment or indicates a grasp of the communicative rituals involved.

4. DISPUTE IT

These activities involve pupils in interrogating the text and evaluating what it has to say.

Pupils could be asked to:

(a) set their own questions on he text – questions which they would like others to consider, either because they don't know the answer at all or because they want to compare their own possible answers with those offered by other pupils;

(b) respond to a series of statements compiled by the teacher which represent a range of (possibly conflicting) views about the text – the statements might be sorted into categories (agree/disagree/don't understand) or arranged into an order of priority;

(c) examine an apparent 'finished' text but one in which imperfections still exist (or have been introduced), looking for and marking up in some way mistakes, inconsistencies, non-sequiturs, etc. – in other words, they are invited to treat the text as a final draft and to put it right.

From: The English Magazine No.11

Chapter 3

Valuing First Languages in Schools

Many teachers and school policies assert that bilingualism is an asset. But what this actually means in principle or practice is not easy to establish from observing what teachers actually do or how schools operate. All too often children are treated as a virtually homogeneous group and those who clearly fall outside the group are either ignored, or they are given 'easy work' or specialist help if it is available.

Most of the research and much of the debate has, as Grosjean (1985) pointed out, been conducted from a monolingual perspective. And yet it is generally agreed that, world-wide, monolingualism is the exception rather than the rule and that operating in at least two languages is a normal aspect of many people's lives. For most British teachers and educational policy makers, however, this is not the case and the supremacy of English both as the medium of education and as a world language make it hard to appreciate the significance of bilingualism.

There are two main aspects to a person's languages. One relates to their identity – personal, social and political. The other concerns the effect on learning concepts and language itself.

Identity

People become bilingual in different ways, for different reasons and at different ages. How they do so may affect their view of themselves and their language. Some grow up in families where two or more languages are spoken as a matter of course. The languages are generally used for different purposes depending on who is being addressed and under what circumstances. It could be that members of the family prefer different languages, for example grandparents may use a different variety from one or both parents. Or religious observance might be conducted in another language. Lambert (1990) refers to this form of bilingualism as compound, where language switching is a common experience from the outset. The other type of bilingualism he identifies is co-ordinate. This 'would be developed through experience in two distinctive linguistic settings' (Lambert, p 204). Language use in the home may, for example, be different from that in the street or at school. Home language could be the majority language, for instance in parts of Wales where Welsh-medium schools are attended by children whose first language is English. More usually in Britain the home language is a minority language.

There are many reasons why people routinely use two or more languages. In diplomatic or business families living in other countries may be a common experience. Families could have moved from their home country because of war or famine, or to change their life-style, to study or to marry. In many long established communities the language of the home remains different from that of the host community for cultural reasons.

Often the second language is only encountered when the child begins to spend time outside the home, at a child-minder, nursery or play-group or in primary school. Sometimes children who have moved from their home country later in life will meet a new language, as well as a new environment, in their teens.

The way in which children see and define themselves may well be influenced by the way in which they acquire their languages and by the attitude of others towards their bilingualism. Blackledge (1994) describes the views that primary children have of themselves as story-tellers and of the stories that they tell in their range of languages. A group of Sylheti speakers felt unable to tell their stories properly in English, saying : 'We won't be able to tell the real story..... I'll have to use some Bengali words.' As Blackledge observes: 'To deny children their language was to deny them their story' (p.49).

If children have learnt that using different languages for appropriate purposes is normal and natural they will find it strange that an important part of their education denies them the opportunity to do so. It also suggests to them that a large part of their experience has no place or value in school.

> To be told, whether directly or indirectly, explicitly or implicitly, that your language and the language of your parents, of your home and of your friends is non-functional in school is to negate your sense of self' (Cummins and Swain, 1986, p. 101).

Savva (1990) writes about Loretta, who speaks Farsi, Armenian and English. Most of her autobiography is written in Farsi, except for that part of it about her history lesson – Henry VII and the Battle of Bosworth Field – which is in English. Evidently this seemed to her the more appropriate language.

The way in which other people respond to one's language is also very important. Osler (in Blackledge, 1994) reports a bilingual teacher who says:

> As soon as I went to school I dropped mother tongue altogether... And I have seen this now with other children. ...But I so wanted to belong. (p.160)

Some children suffer racist taunts because of the way they speak. Others change their language use in order to identify more closely with their peers.

> Occasionally my mother would correct my speech when speaking Greek, telling me that if I spoke and wrote Greek with a Cypriot dialect, people would think I was a peasant (quoted in the African-Caribbean Language and Literacy Project).

> Knowing his maternal language helps a man to know himself; being proud of his language helps a man to be proud of himself. The Indian people are expressing concern that the native languages are being lost, that the younger generations can no longer speak or understand their mother tongue. If the Indian identity is to be preserved, steps must be taken to reverse this trend (Skutnabb-Kangas, 1981).

> If I speak about the mosque or about religion, the Muslim religion, or I speak about Morocco, I feel much better if I speak it in Arabic (Miller, 1983).

Language has a social and political dimension as well as a personal one. The status of a nation or group is reflected in the value accorded to its language. Thus speakers of European languages are generally admired for their bilingual abilities and children may even be sent to schools which offer advanced skills in French, German or Italian. The fluency with which many European public figures speak English as well as their own and possibly other foreign languages is quite properly respected. The justification for the Modern Foreign Language Curriculum offering French, German or Spanish is largely an economic one. Much less status is given to speakers who use Turkish, Urdu or Gujerati in their daily lives I our cities and communities and very limited opportunities are offered to pupils who wish to improve their fluency and gain qualifications in their first language.

The reasons for this lie in part within our own history. When the British colonised and plundered other parts of the world they brought with them their 'civilisation' in the form of British customs and traditions, Christianity and the English language. Even though Europeans could be said to have helped create Creoles through the importation of West Africans from diverse language groups as slaves to the Caribbean, the contempt with which they regarded speakers of these tongues remains in our institutions to this day. Many people still dismiss non-European languages as 'gibberish', written in a peculiar 'scrawl' and sometimes even 'back to front'! While this attitude might not be widespread in our schools, it will nonetheless have been encountered by many of our pupils.

Racism in British society is well documented. Black people, many of whom were actively recruited to fill job vacancies in the transport and health services, often suffer discrimination in employment and housing. Social attitudes towards them compound negative feelings about the languages they speak and if groups are unable to mix freely or willingly they lose opportunities to learn about one another's culture and customs.

Language has always been a political issue. Lives have been lost in the struggle to assert national identity through demanding recognition for their languages. In South Africa the 1976 Soweto uprisings were, at least in part, about the language in which Black South Africans wished to be educated. The Bantu Education Act of 1954 had changed the language of education from English to 'mother tongue', in which there were few books or resources. In the 70s this policy was changed again when it was decreed that some subjects should be taught in Afrikaans, the language of the oppressors, spoken by very few African teachers. Hector Pieterson was only the first of many young people to be killed when police opened fire on a peaceful demonstration by school students demanding not Afrikaans but English-medium education.

In Bangladesh February 21st 1952 is commemorated as the date when a group, who became known as the Language Martyrs, were shot while protesting at the East Pakistani government's attempt to enforce the use of Urdu rather than Bengali. Independence in 1972 ensured self-determination in language.

Language is not neutral. It is part of our definition of who we are and can affect the attitudes of other people towards us. The way in which we use our languages is a product and a determinant of this identity. To deny language in education, therefore, is to deny a part of the learner.

Learning and bilingualism

Being bilingual can have tremendous advantages not only in terms of language competencies, but also in terms of cognitive and social development (Lambert, 1990, p.210).

There is now considerable research evidence that bilingualism is not a hindrance but an advantage in terms of learning as well as meta-linguistic skills. Bilingual learners have greater flexibility and creativity in their learning. They also seem to be better at problem solving. This seems to apply to bilinguals from a wide range of linguistic groups. Many of the studies which provide the evidence were conducted by psychologists under laboratory conditions. But there have also been a number of studies which evaluate educational programmes in two or more languages, many of them from Canada and Sweden but also a few from Britain.

In 1976 Bedfordshire Education Authority set up a project, funded by the EEC, to evaluate the benefits of using mother tongue as a medium of education. Panjabi and Italian language and culture were taught to groups of pupils for approximately 5 hours each week. The project ran for four years, although not all the children were involved throughout. In addition to their teaching responsibilities staff involved in the project also produced materials and developed school-home liaison.

The project had many interesting outcomes, not least of which was the debate about whether to teach standard versions of the language or the dialects with which the children were more familiar. The attitude of pupils to learning their first language in school compared favourably with those who went to extra classes outside school which they saw as a chore, 'not good enough for real school'. It was found that children who participated in the programme not only gained confidence in their first language,but they also achieved in their overall learning. Learning in L1 did not inhibit, but rather seemed to benefit, learning in L2.

In 1978 the Mother Tongue and English Teaching Project (MOTET) was set up in Bradford. Rising five year-olds, entering school speaking little or no English, were taught in both Panjabi and English. Their achievements were compared with a control group taught entirely in English. The aim of the project was to evaluate the use of mother tongue as part of educational achievement in English. It was not designed to justify first language education. As might be expected, competence in Panjabi was noticeably better for the first group but, interestingly there was no reduction in their English language skills nor their cognitive development.

These and many similar studies in North America and Europe suggest the existence of what Cummins has called a 'common underlying proficiency'. He suggests that the ability to use language to convey meaning, the ability to formulate rules in order to string words together, and other language skills such as literacy, are independent of the actual language being used. So children who have understood a concept in one language do not have to relearn it in another; their understanding is transferable. They may still have preferences about which language to use in any given situation and may still have to learn the vocabulary in which to express their knowledge but they do not have to relearn the concepts. Loretta could have written about the Battle of Bosworth Field in Farsi had she known the vocabulary.

This debate raises questions about the relationship between language and thought. Language is the main medium through which we categorise reality and the words that we use may reflect our understanding of the world. But that understanding can be expressed, however clumsily, in any language. To use a classic example, English may not have such an elegant way of describing light, dry, powdery snow as Inuit languages, but it can be used to express the same concept.

In response to the interest in bilingualism the Department of Education and Science funded the Linguistic Minorities Project (see Stubbs, 1985). It reported in 1983, publishing a full account of the 'other languages of England' and describing the distribution and variety of languages spoken in England and the provision for their maintenance (Stubbs, 1985). The project built on the investigation by Rosen and Burgess (1980) into the languages and dialects of London schoolchildren.

In 1985 the Swann Committee published its final report *Education For All* (Swann, 1985) which had taken evidence from many individuals and institutions about the causes of under-achievement in the ethnic minority community. Swann makes reference to the 1977 EC Directive on the Education of Children of Migrant Workers which states that Member States should make provision for the 'teaching of the mother tongue and culture of the country of origin' of all children of compulsory school age who are dependents of workers from Member States. The Swann Committee took this to mean 'with a view principally to facilitating their possible reintegration into the Member State of origin' (Swann, p.401). Mother tongue teaching was seen by the committee as being the responsibility of the community and at best of transitional value.

If children are taught in a language that they can understand they are more likely to learn than if they have to learn a new language and make sense of new concepts at the same time. Most bilingual learners in Britain, however, are expected to cope with both at once.

Provision

There are basically two different kinds of bilingual programme. Transitional bilingualism refers to the use of first language, often in the early years, as educational support until the pupil is able to operate effectively in the second language. The message indicated by this sort of support is that the first language is of lesser importance. Monoliterate bilingual programmes, one form of transitional provision, encourage the development of oral skills in both languages but limit literacy to the second and more prestigious language. Effectively this limits the use and status of first language to non-academic activities. Children use different languages to talk about different subjects so if reading and writing, central to school, only take place in the second language, then talk in first language is likely to be restricted.

Group or bilingual maintenance programmes aim to develop literacy as well as oral skills in both languages. Some programmes do this simultaneously in all subjects and some divide the timetable between subjects taught in L1 and those that use L2. Ideally, both languages are taught as subjects in their own right as well as being used equally as mediums of education. It has been found that learning is most effective when both languages are used to develop conceptual understanding.and that this approach has a beneficial effect on first language use in the home and community.

Although there have been many different local attempts to meet the need (see for example Rosen and Burgess, 1980, Houlton and Willey, 1983 and Robinson, 1985), most take the form of transitional programmes and few have been systematically evaluated. Our views of bilingualism have moved from deficit theories, which saw multiple language use as confusing, to difference theories, which have a more liberal feel. These affirm bilingual language development as possible without interference or confusion between one language and the other. However, even difference theories can disguise a deficit view and even where they are genuine, often call for change on the part of the minority communities whose differences are seen as causing a problem to themselves and the schools.

Change must occur in schools if the rhetoric is to become a reality. In the words of Genesee, 1994 we must:

> encourage the development of the home language and culture both in the homes of language minority children and, where possible, in their schools and use the linguistic, cognitive and sociocultural resources that language minority children bring to school as a basis for planning their formal education (p.7).

Or, as Whitehead (1990) observes: 'To exclude a language is to exclude its speakers' (p 85).

Heath (1983), in her detailed study of language development in two communities in the USA, describes the effect that different traditions and customs have on the early educational achievements of children. She devotes the second part of her book to a discussion of how teachers as learners and learners as ethnographers can build on what they observe and learn about language use in schools and classrooms. By learners Heath means both pupils and teachers and she argues that unless links can be made between community language and school language teachers expectations are limited and children's opportunities are restricted.

There is a continuum that stretches from 'valuing first language' to 'teaching community languages' in the practical steps that we can take in our schools and classrooms.

Valuing first language

At the absolute minimum, we need to show all children that what they bring to school has a place and a value. Signs and notices in languages other than English are becoming common in many schools and are now available commercially. Several companies and LEAs publish 'Welcome' posters. The choice of languages need not be restricted to those in the school community but can give the wider message that communication is not confined to the English language. But if the gesture stops there it gives only a very limited and utilitarian view of diversity.

Dual-text books

An increasing number of publishers are meeting a demand for dual-text books. These were, and generally remain, translations of English picture books and traditional stories for young children. The English text is usually followed by the other language, although in more recent publications the order is sometimes reversed. In most books both scripts are printed although in earlier versions the English was printed and the additional language sometimes hand-written. There are a few books in which the use of two languages is integral to the story but usually the same, or a similar, text appears in both languages, a device which is most unusual in 'normal' literature.

We need to ask ourselves a number of questions about dual-text books, most fundamentally, what are our reasons for using them? Some would argue that it gives status to other languages, but that is largely to promote language awareness for the monolingual pupils. Bilingual learners and their parents are far more likely to take this attempt to accord status seriously if a good range of books written in the first language were provided alongside the English books.

It has been argued that it helps children to learn the English if they can read or hear their parents or other adults read a first language version of the story. Familiarity with the story is one of the cues that readers bring to a text but beyond this there is very little evidence that direct comparison is or indeed could be made. Translations are rarely word for word so although the gist of the story may be the same, details are often different. Translation is very difficult to do and the choice of words is often a matter of judgement and cultural connotation. Evidence suggests that readers are likely to choose to read the version in the language in which they are most fluent and ignore the other. This certainly seems to be so in the case of spoken language. Fillmore

(1980) videotaped children in a bilingual instruction classroom and observed that they listened only to the language that they understood best. However, Ming Tsow (1986) gives an example in a case study of how the stronger language can support the weaker:

> ...it seems that the stronger language – English – helps the child to prepare the internal text. By the use of approximation, mental and linguistic from one language to another, she gradually shifts to Bengali competence.

One of the chief reasons for using dual-text books may well be because monolingual teachers need to feel they have access to the reading material.

> The main benefit is for the teachers so that they will know what the story's about. I can't see the bilingual children benefiting because they are more likely to read the English. Many of them have learnt to read English first and can't read their mother tongue so it's not providing access to literacy in their first language. (Kumar, 1988)

There may, nevertheless, be good reasons for choosing dual-text books, not least if children or parents ask for them. Feuerverger (1994) suggests that the use of such books can help to build partnerships between parents and teachers and improve 'intercultural' relations but we need to be discriminating in our selection. The two texts should be scrutinised to see if they are given equal status. This is particularly difficult in languages such as Arabic, Urdu, Hebrew or Farsi, which are written from right to left. Where should such a book start? Illustrations need to relate to both texts. We should also check that the authors and translators are acknowledged and if possible seek advice about the quality of the translation. Ultimately we might decide that single text books are preferable. As one bilingual Section 11 teacher commented: 'Community language teachers would prefer to have a good range of books in the community language. They don't necessarily need or want an English translation.'

The subject matter also needs to be scrutinised. For older children it is useful to provide non-fiction and original texts in a range of languages rather than to rely on translations of English books. If dual-text books are restricted to picture books and fables it conveys a very distorted message of literature in other languages. Bilingual learners have a right to a wide range of books that reflect their culture and interests.

We must also consider how first language books are to be arranged and catalogued. In some schools and libraries, not least in public libraries, texts in languages other than English are separated from the rest. If they are put in a separate section they are unlikely even to serve a language awareness function.

One undoubted benefit that dual-text books have had is to promote the making of books in several languages in schools. Children use their languages for a real purpose and audience and often involve their parents and others in the production. Pupils might write their autobiographies in first language, with or without a translation in English. This can be extended to using linguistic diversity in making labels, games, instructions and other materials. With the increasing availability of laminators, binders and computer programs in different scripts, the results look very professional.

Specialist publishers are the main producers of resources in first languages and a list of where they can be purchased should be part of the information in every school. Publishers and distributors have shown that they are capable of providing books in other languages if the demand is there. We need to create a demand for the sort of books which are of educational value.

Using first languages in schools

A more active response to first language is to use it in the classroom. A simple start can be made in the form of greetings. It is not much trouble to learn some of the phrases that our pupils use for greetings. Some primary teachers take the register by welcoming their pupils in various ways. In secondary schools teachers can learn some basic instructions and requests, most readily from the pupils themselves, indicating that other languages are to be welcomed and encouraging their use in real situations.

Resources to promote use include the many story tapes now available as well as alphabet charts, equipment posters and instruction sheets in languages other than English. Some of these are produced commercially, others by schools or LEA Section 11 teams.

Monolingual teachers are sometimes concerned that they will not understand what is being said or written if pupils do not use English. It is not always necessary, or possible, for us to overhear everything and often the most productive learning takes place when pupils have the freedom to discuss ideas and make suggestions independently of the teacher. We can usually judge when pupils are on task and purposeful talk is evident from its outcomes.

Pupils, particularly in secondary schools, may be literate in their first languages. This of enormous benefit to them in developing literacy skills in English, and writing in first language should always be encouraged. Children may wish to make personal notes or to write a first draft in their stronger language. They can often explain and translate the gist of what they have written, even if their level of English does not yet equip them to do a full translation. An example of the benefit of encouraging writing in the first language was provided by a recently arrived Vietnamese student in Yr 11. She was writing a fairly structured and straightforward autobiography as part of her English course work and was clearly frustrated at her inability to express her deeper feelings in English. She wrote a poem in Vietnamese and, several months later when she was more fluent in English, translated it for the teacher. The pupil's expressive ability was only then revealed to the teacher.

Similarly, a Turkish boy in junior school wrote about a science experiment in Turkish, complete with labels for the diagrams. This served as a record for him about his own learning and enabled him to to talk about it with the teacher so that she found out what he had understood. At a later stage the teacher managed to get a translation from a colleague which confirmed her assessment of the pupil's ability.

Interpreters and translators can help to encourage pupils to use their first languages. Curtis (1992) recommends the use of peer tutoring, in which more experienced bilingual pupils support newcomers in their learning. She found that, particularly in subjects where the emphasis was on practical and oral skills, the use of the first language enhanced the learning of both pupils.

Bilingual teachers and assistants, often employed in Section 11 projects, work in a variety of ways. In authorities where there are few bilingual learners, or a large number of different languages are spoken, they are often organised into peripatetic teams. This enables them to visit as many children as possible during the course of a week or term. Such teachers often see themselves, and are seen by schools and teachers, as support for the children, rather than collaborators with teachers or curriculum advisors. This can have negative effects on their status and, in the case of those who have trained and qualified abroad, is often confirmed by lack of QTS or career opportunities.

We need to ensure that we include all staff in the decisions that affect the pupils. We need to consult and plan together and draw on their knowledge and observations. Mills (1994) has indicated the range of skills that bilingual assistants bring to the classroom, classifying them as educational, pastoral and liaison. She points out that they are often able to do work that classteachers are unable to fulfil, such as talking to parents in home languages, interpreting for other professionals such as social workers and doctors, telling stories in first language and comforting children who cannot explain why they are upset. By working with bilingual adults in a professional manner we provide models of respect to our pupils as well as enabling them to make fuller use of their first languages.

Promoting first language in schools

We need to know what languages are spoken in the school if we are to promote their use. The importance of information gathering at the admission stage has already been stressed. Pupils can be involved in discovering more about language diversity as already happens in some schools. Some use the Linguistic Minorities Project survey (see Stubbs, 1985) or an adaptation of it, others have developed their own methods.

The National Curriculum, while providing an opportunity for language awareness, gives no guidance on the necessity or place of the study of linguistic diversity. In 1982 the Commission for Racial Equality was suggesting that a language education programme should have several aspects:

a) an awareness of the linguistic diversity of Britain's multi-racial society;

b) a knowledge of both the cultural and linguistic characteristics of these languages;

c) a recognition that these languages should have a place in formal education;

d) a basic knowledge of some of the misconceptions about bilingual education. (CRE, 1982 p 10)

Increasingly teachers are seeing the value of language awareness in promoting understanding and respect for all the languages of the pupils and helping to maintain crucial links between the school and the community. In one infant school it was decided to 'grow' a language tree. Each pupil was given a paper leaf to write their name on and, with the help of parents, the languages that they used. These were decorated and placed on an enormous 'trunk' in the main hall. Parents were invited to an assembly which was held to celebrate the completion of the tree and the impressive number of languages represented. The teachers' fears that some children and parents might deny using languages other than English were allayed as parents felt empowered to decide their own language repertoire. More African-Caribbean parents than expected identified their own Creole languages, partly because they were aware that the school took a positive view of bilingualism.

Such shared knowledge about language can stimulate curiosity about differences in writing systems and vocabulary. Children enjoy watching and experimenting with different forms of writing and are often full of admiration for their friends' ability to write and read unfamiliar scripts. Chinese or Arabic, for example, can be appreciated aesthetically, from the nursery onwards.

> A popular activity in one nursery class during Chinese New Year was writing scrolls with the greeting 'Happy New Year' in Cantonese. All the children were keen to have a go and they took great concentration and care, using fine black felt tips to copy the symbols... In this activity we were all equally learners, and Chinese children and parents were the teachers. (Burgess-Macey, 1994)

Similarly work on the movement of peoples and their languages, the effects on English vocabulary of contact with other cultures and the differences in how people use language can be of great interest to pupils. Work such as this falls under the heading of 'language awareness', developed, often in secondary Modern Languages Departments, to introduce pupils to language study (see Hawkins, 1984). Some of these approaches have been criticised as tokenistic, and indeed some courses aimed to be just that, providing 'tasters' in several languages before the main one was studied. More recently language awareness has included discussion about the power and status of languages as part of the exploration of how they are used.

Waheed (1992) describes a series of lessons she planned for a Yr 9 class. One girl was looking at the way in which language could be used to define group identity, and sometimes to exclude, and wrote about an episode on a bus when she and a friend talked in Panjabi about another passenger. She had written 'The lady looked back at me and then turned the cigarette off' and later in discussing her work noticed the way she had used Panjabi phraseology in an English sentence.

Issues of power need not be confined to secondary pupils. Children in the early years have a strong sense of justice and an understanding about how inequalities operate. They can talk, from their own observations and experience, about how young people are spoken to, the differences in the way in which men and women or parents and teachers address one another and the use of different languages in conversations with other people. Talking about different houses in their neighbourhood led a group of juniors into a more general discussion of the sorts of people who live in different types of homes. They matched pictures of houses to their supposed occupants and then made up a 'typical' dialogue for each. Issues of speech and dialect – who talks 'posh' and why – were spontaneously explored.

The pupils and their communities are an important resource and many schools now have bilingual staff who can also contribute to promoting first languages. Members of the community – musicians, athletes, business people – are often delighted to share their knowledge with pupils and should be encouraged to do so in first languages where possible. Even if the languages used are not familiar to every pupil the act of discovering and talking about them signals that language is a worthy topic of interest and study. We need, however, to be sensitive in the ways in which we 'exploit' bilingual parents and colleagues. Too often ethnic minority parents are invited to share the 'exotic' as if story-telling or cooking are all they can contribute. Bilingual skills should be valued, but this should be in the context of the other abilities that parents and helpers wish to share with our children. We may be stereotyping people if we only ask them to become involved in festivals.

Bilingual staff can feel undervalued. As one bilingual Section 11 teacher remarks, it is disheartening when they are 'only used for making translations. Then the teaching element can disappear. They will be helping the teacher and not the children' Bilingual teachers and classroom assistants usually want to be considered first and foremost as educators. It is unfortunate that because of the discrimination they suffer in getting employment and recognition many are being channelled into Section 11 posts. We, and our children, need more bilingual primary classteachers and secondary science, history and maths teachers.

In many classrooms there are several different languages spoken and it would be unusual to find a teacher or bilingual classroom assistant who was fluent in all of them. A teacher who has experience of using several languages is more sensitive to communicative issues in the classroom whether or not all children share her/his languages.

'Sometimes I am reinforcing the English language through Punjabi or Urdu. Sometimes I will issue instructions or commands in their mother tongue... but I won't only say it to the bilingual children. Often I say to Gary, 'chup' (quiet) and he knows the meaning of the Punjabi. (quoted in Sidhu, 1993 p.132)

In most classrooms the medium of instruction is English, but some of the best practice in promoting first languages involves the use of two languages to teach as well as learn. Bilingual teachers can do this naturally. Those of us who are lucky enough to collaborate with bilingual teachers, assistants or helpers should plan to use both languages as much as possible. It is only by showing that we respect languages and that all languages are equally capable of being used to express ideas, feelings and explanations that bilingual pupils will feel able to use them in their learning.

Teaching first languages in schools

Bilingual maintenance programmes not only value, use and promote first languages, they would also teach them as a subject in their own right. The Commission for Racial Equality report of 1982 provides arguments for teaching first language within the education system. The Swann Report (1985) saw community languages as the responsibility of minority communities, thus reinforcing resistance to promoting linguistic diversity. The Swann Report argues that first language learning is only of relevance to ethnic minority pupils, who would therefore need separate provision. This the report deems to be contrary to principles of equality.

> On the contrary, the key to equality of opportunity, to academic success and, more broadly, to participation on equal terms as a full member of society, is good command of English and the emphasis must therefore we feel be on the learning of English (Swann, 1985 para 3.16).

The CRE recommends that community languages could be taught to native first language speakers and to non-speakers as a foreign language. They could also be used directly as a medium of education in bilingual programmes. There are several practical difficulties to this policy, but these alone should not prevent its consideration.

One common objection is over which language(s) to teach. The National Curriculum requires schools to offer at least one European language. The choice of which community language to timetable in addition must be decided by the school. Sometimes this is resolved pragmatically in the light of existing resources. Some schools have a particular expert available, others have links with another institution or an embassy which can provide a language teacher. There are also objections on the grounds that choosing one language discriminates against all the others. However, just because we cannot do everything we should not be deterred from doing something.

Decisions about how to timetable first language classes are not easy. The take-up of Gujerati at one secondary school was surprisingly low considering the population and the initial interest, but it transpired that parents were unwilling to allow their daughters to stay after school and travel home on their own and, in winter, in the dark. Some schools timetable first language classes against other more prestigious subjects, or as an extra which pupils study in their own time. In primary schools the issue can become one of withdrawal from the mainstream curriculum.

Thought needs to be given to which pupils might be expected to take up community languages. In some schools all subjects are offered to all students, whether native-speakers or not. Greatly different levels of fluency, particularly of literacy, make demands on teachers and some teachers may insist on a certain initial level of proficiency. For some students traditional 'foreign language' pedagogies may be inappropriate and different teaching methods may need to be tried. This could have implications for teacher training and professional development. Tosi (1988) points out that principles of equality of opportunity are at issue. If by equality one means treating everyone equally the rights of bilingual learners to have their native linguistic competence recognised and developed could be at stake.

Learners who are already bilingual are likely to be more receptive to other foreign languages and are often keen to learn one of the traditional European languages. The methods and texts used are unlikely to stimulate or interest them any more than they do most native English speakers. The cultures represented in most standard texts are uniformly white and middle class. Reliance in many classes on English rather than on communicative competence in the target language can disadvantage some bilingual pupils.

Despite the problems of transport and time many pupils continue to learn their first languages in complementary and supplementary schools., many of them long-established and run on a voluntary basis. Some are attached to temples or mosques, others concentrate on teaching language and culture and others provide additional teaching in National Curriculum subjects. As Khan (1994) points out: 'These efforts by the community to educate their own youngsters are indications of the deep desire both to fulfil their educational needs and to exert their self identity' (p. 20). Voluntary schools are an important part of the learner's experience and should be acknowledged as such by teachers, not least because of the time and effort that pupils devote to them.

Direct input, in English plus a community language, has been a very successful technique in some schools. Where bilingual teachers are appointed and the school recognises the value in developing first language skills and not merely in providing a transitional bilingual programme, there are benefits in terms of learning and language development Some primary schools in areas with large numbers of bilingual learners already draw on both languages in teaching. One or two secondary schools have used languages other than English systematically in subject teaching, but such practice is rare.

Bilingualism will only become a reality if the curriculum reflects its use and value. And this can only happen when the role of first language in learning is understood. This has implications for policy, teacher training, the National Curriculum and public attitudes. The evidence is available; the debate needs to reach a wider audience.

Chapter 4

New School, New Language

Language in home and school

For the majority of children, arrival in school presents them with new linguistic demands and experiences. Bernstein, although he claims to have been misrepresented, has been taken to suggest the existence of two distinct codes of English language use. The restricted code, typical of working class families, deals effectively with the concrete, here-and-now and is less susceptible to expressions of abstract thought. The elaborated code, which is that used largely by middle class families and demanded by schooling, is more context-free and impersonal and therefore more suitable for discussing abstractions and ideas.

Whatever the interpretation placed on Bernstein's work, he certainly pointed to a distinction that lies within the experience of many teachers and parents, namely the differences between language use at home and school. As Halliday states (1978):

> Education as at present organised demanded elaborated code; therefore, if any social group had, by virtue of its patterns of socialisation, only partial or conditional control over this code, that group would be at a disadvantage. (p.87)

These differences were graphically demonstrated by several research studies. Tizard and Hughes (1984) studied the language use of a small group of 4-year old girls both at home and in the nursery school. One of their explicit aims was to discover the extent to which 'working class' language is inadequate for schooling and specifically for logical thought. They found that although there may be differences in emphasis between working class and middle class homes, there was no evidence of language deficit. In all homes in this study the children and their mothers engaged in a wide range of language activities. The development of English was sustained by the interest and involvement of the adult, and by the practical activities in which they were jointly concerned.

A longitudinal study of a larger number of children, the Bristol study, has been reported on over a period of years. In *The Meaning Makers*, Wells (1986) described the differences between language used in the home and the school. He and his team investigated the language used by native English speaking children in different contexts. He found that by the age of five children from all social backgrounds are fluent and confident users of language. They understand conversational conventions and use language for a wide variety of purposes.

Interestingly, this fluency was not always evident at school and teachers perceived some children as linguistically deprived. Wells describes Rosie, a 5-year old, interacting with two different teachers. With one she is unresponsive and mono-syllabic, despite the apparent advantage of having a practical activity to talk about. In contrast, when discussing her reading book with the second teacher, Rosie is vivacious and eloquent, initiating conversation and extending her ideas. It would not be surprising if the first teacher had any low expectations of working class children confirmed by her interaction with Rosie.

Heath (1983) observed and compared the child-rearing practices, attitudes, learning and language use in a white and a black working class community in the United States. She found significant differences between them in, for instance, their attitude to talk, their use of stories and their reading practices. The discontinuities between home and school were a major cause of lack of achievement in the essentially white and middle class practice and expectations of the school.

Experiences of reading will also vary considerably and are often very diverse. Children will, for example, have read and seen the different uses of sacred texts, mail order catalogues and newspapers, reference books and re-creational literature.

Teachers' attitudes to languages will affect their reactions and expectations to language use and proficiency. Labov (1969) describes the differences that the situation and the interaction can make both to the quality of utterances and to the assessment of them. He was particularly interested in the negative attitudes associated with Black English Vernacular and shows that it is as rich and logical a language as the standard form.

Judgements about the thought processes and ability of children who use non-standard varieties can have serious and long-term effects. Coard (1971) was concerned at the misidentification of 'West Indian' children as having Special Educational Needs. On the basis of judgements made about their language proficiency, assumptions were made about their cognitive abilities which led to these pupils being wrongly placed in Special Schools.

Cummins (1984) investigated precisely the same phenomenon in the case of bilingual learners, mainly in the United States and Canada. His starting point was the concern about the 'disproportionate numbers of immigrant and minority language children 'deported' into special education classes and vocational streams in many countries ' (p.1).

He concluded that part of the difficulty lay in the unexamined assumptions about the processes of teaching and learning and in particular about assessment, that were not shared between home and school. This mismatch resulted, he argued, in the inaccurate and inappropriate assessment of bilingual learners whose language and learning styles did not match teacher expectations.

Cummins argued for teaching styles to alter in order to give learners more control over, and active involvement in, their learning. He also called for a change in the approach to assessment to one which relied less on 'psycho-educational' testing and more on longitudinal observation and sampling. Finally he urged more representation and information about children's home language and culture within the school context.

Importantly, Cummins has placed the debate in a political context, arguing that failure to acknowledge the achievements of bilingual learners and the success of bilingual educational programmes is, at least in part, due to racism and entrenched attitudes on the part of decision-makers.

Politics of language

Linguistic and cultural diversity is not a new phenomenon in British classrooms and has always had a political dimension. The history of English is the history of invasion, colonialisation and migration. In different parts of the

British Isles different languages and dialects have always been present and attempts by those in control of the education system to suppress or change indigenous languages is a old as the education system itself.

In the 16th century children who spoke English, rather than Latin, in school were punished. Similarly, in the 19th century, Welsh speaking pupils were forced to wear a wooden plaque if overheard using their native language instead of English. There are still occasional reports of teachers telling children to 'Stop jabbering. Speak English'.

Responses to this diversity have changed. During the period roughly described as 'assimilationist', in 1960s and 1970s, the educational reaction to linguistic diversity was one of remediation. As a largely monolingual community, British teachers thought that bilingualism was an exotic and probably confusing experience and that non-standard usage should be corrected.

Many of the 'non-English-speakers' that teachers came into contact with were immigrants and it was not thought important that teachers know anything about the languages that they used at home or in the community. Indeed, the first language was thought to interfere with the necessary development of English and ethnic minority parents were urged to speak English to their children.

In order to facilitate the use of English, 'non-English-speakers', sometimes even referred to as having 'no language', were withdrawn from the mainstream for part or all of their education. This was not in order to enable greater use of their first language in the English acquisition process but simply to practice and drill learners in the new language, ignoring or suppressing their first language. It was thought that until they had learnt English to a fluency sufficient to participate in mainstream no conceptual learning could take place. Yetta Goodman, writing only 10 years ago, said that: 'Attitudes such as 'these children have no language' or 'bilingualism confuses children' are still too prevalent' (Goodman, 1985).

In 1975 the Bullock Report (1975) recognised the importance of first languages. The much quoted passage: 'No child should be expected to cast off the language and culture of the home as he (sic) crosses the school threshold, nor to live and act as though school and home represent two totally separate and different cultures which have to be kept firmly apart' (p.286) is still relevant today and many teachers are concerned about how to make this intention a reality.

The 1980s saw a shift towards cultural pluralism. The Swann Report (1985) encouraged the education of bilingual learners in the mainstream and the so-called Calderdale Report (CRE, 1986) drew attention to the racist nature of withdrawal.

Attitudes towards language diversity seemed to be concerned with co-operation and celebration. The value of bilingualism had, at least in the rhetoric, been recognised. Educationally this manifested itself in a greater tolerance of first language use, at least as a transitional phase and the realisation that errors, as in first language development, were an important part of the learning process. The term 'interlanguage' was used for the process by which learners experiment with aspects of both the strongest and the new language in order to form a transitional system with its own internal consistency. 'Errors' were not only tolerated but recognised as part of the acquisition process, illuminating in much the same way as miscue analysis sees the errors in reading as a window onto the reading process.

The co-operative aspect was seen in the changing role of the support teacher, who was now no longer the absent expert whose job was to prepare bilingual learners for the educational life of the classroom but an in-class professional whose main role was to make the curriculum accessible to bilingual learners. Part of this involved making assessments of the levels of English fluency of bilingual learners so that mainstream colleagues could have more informed and realistic expectations and possibly make provision for pupils when support was not available.

Celebration often took the form of a multicultural response to the curriculum. In secondary schools in particular, Black studies and language awareness courses were developed. In primary schools a wider range of resources were seen in the classroom. Publishers responded with an increasing number of 'multicultural' titles and often produced specialist lists to guide and simplify choice.

An interesting aspect of the cultural pluralism approach included the beginnings of a changing attitude to Creole languages and African-Caribbean pupils. If linguistic and cultural diversity was to be celebrated then this ought to include the dialects and languages of all pupils. The debate about the status of Creoles as languages continues but with increasing recognition that Creoles are distinctive languages and not 'bad' or 'sloppy' English.

However it is evident that celebrating cultural diversity does not in itself achieve equality nor raise levels of attainment. We are perhaps entering a new phase in both educational politics and practice. In some respects teachers are encouraging independence and individuality and are recognising that children bring their own unique experiences which form a vital part of their identity and learning. The particular contributions and strengths of bilingual learners are better understood and documented and are beginning to inform educational practice. We recognise that pupils need to be more involved in decisions that affect their own learning and that cognitive and linguistic development are intimately related and cannot continue independently.

At the same time we are becoming increasingly aware of the negative aspects of the emphasis on independence and individuality as manifested in racist politics and practice. Competitiveness between LEAs, schools and teachers and pressures from, amongst other things, the National Curriculum, can affect the level of co-operation within the classroom.

Responding to diversity

Like all children, bilingual learners arrive in school, at whatever stage in their education, with a range of abilities and experiences to build on. They come with an identity and personality, a personal history and experiences, a culture including language(s) and an education, whether formal or informal.

The most obvious aspects of a person's identity are their gender, race and colour. But even these are open to interpretation and elicit varied and often stereotyped responses.

Gender seems to be the most straightforward. It is not always possible to determine a child's gender from their name and in several cultures, including 'British', some names can be used for both boys and girls. Equally, parents' names and titles may not give an immediate indication to the uninformed about their gender. We need to learn from the parents and community themselves.

Most societies expect boys and girls to behave differently, but these expectations change across time and from individual to individual and it is dangerous to make any assumptions based on gender. Increasingly, members of ethnic minority communities are challenging views about, for example, dominant Muslim men or passive Asian girls. What teachers are entitled to do is make clear in our behaviour and discussions what we expect of boys and girls in the classroom and around the school. We may need to explain this carefully to both pupils and parents but we need not flinch from setting standards of equality of treatment and respect.

It is rare to find a school that is still so rigid in its uniform regulations that it will not accommodate the requirements of some Muslim girls to wear trousers, for example, or allow Sikh boys to wear turbans if they so wish. Similar sensitivity is also necessary in respect of PE, swimming, dance etc.

The issue of *race* and colour is a sensitive one. A growing number of education authorities are collecting statistics which include racial or ethnic origin. Home Office guidelines suggest the importance of self-identification, but then go on to propose a curious set of categories that respondents might use. These include Black-Caribbean, Black-African, White and also Bangladeshi, Indian, Pakistani. It is not at all clear that these are mutually exclusive groups and they seem to confuse ethnicity, 'race' and nationality.

The concept of race is largely discredited in biological terms as applied to humans. It has been used scientifically to describe certain physical characteristics that identify and separate groups. Genetic variation in humans has been widely studied and it is generally accepted that differences within so-called races are as great as differences between them. As Thorp (1991) observes: 'We would argue that 'race' was a social construct used primarily to justify discriminatory practices '(p.176). Biological definitions of 'race' certainly have a poor history, being connected with notions of racial purity and other subtler forms of racism.

However, the concept of race or colour is also widely used in a political sense, chiefly in terms of 'Black' and 'White'. It is useful to be able to identify groups of people who have common experiences of discrimination and racism, as against those who are part of the powerful groups in society. Wherever possible people's preferences should be respected, for example some Asians refer to themselves as Black in order to identify with other oppressed groups. Others prefer to be known as Asian or Indian. Many Turkish speakers, whether from mainland Turkey or Cyprus, identify as 'Black', though in terms of skin colour others may perceive them as 'White'.

However terms such as race, colour or ethnicity are used, it is important to clarify their meaning and to respect the wishes of those who are being so classified. It is of interest for all of us to reflect on how we might identify ourselves in terms of these categories. Those of us who are 'White, British' are rarely asked to do so.

The question of *names* has been referred to above in relation to gender. A person's name is a significant part of their identity, linking them as it does with their family and history. Some names have very specific and personal meanings. We are all aware of how the misuse of names can be hurtful and abusive and should take the greatest care to establish the correct spelling and pronunciation of names of both pupils and their parents. We should always ask about family names and titles and not make assumptions based on a Western tradition. Names from cultures which use a non-Roman script will have had to be transcribed so similar names may well have different spellings, for example Najma can also be written Najmah.

Some pupils Anglicise their names for a variety of reasons. If the main reason is mispronunciation on the part of teachers then this should be rectified. However, there may be other reasons, for example a desire on the part of parents to change their identity or a wish by a teenager to be accepted by a particular peer group. Whatever the pressures the individual's wishes should be respected.

Personality is an important aspect of learning. We all have different ways of learning and of relating to other people. We all have different views of ourselves as individuals. Our reactions to situations depend not only on the situations themselves and the other people involved in them but also on our individuality. Personal characteristics need to be accommodated within the classroom as far as possible. We should not make assumptions about pupils' behaviour based on their gender or ethnic background but give them space and opportunity to define themselves.

Equally we should not make assumptions about 'self-esteem'. African-Caribbean pupils in particular are sometimes accused of having 'low self-esteem'. These judgements by teachers are often based on what they see as unacceptable or non-conforming behaviour or low attainment. In either case it is always difficult to impute motives or feelings to others and often more productive to look for other reasons to account for particular reactions. In some cases it may be that pupils are displaying a rejection of low expectations, or of the values and objectives of a system which they experience as alienating. Frequently it is not low 'self' esteem but the low value that teachers and the education system places on black pupils and their achievements that provide the explanation.

The *history and experiences* that children bring with them to the classroom will also affect their learning. Bilingual learners come from a wide range of backgrounds and have diverse personal histories. Some will be second or third generation British, whose families are part of well established local communities Others will be recent arrivals whose circumstances are uncertain and insecure. Some will maintain links with countries of origin, returning frequently to visit friends and families, and will have strong emotive ties. Others may have experienced pain, dislocation and rejection and see Britain as a haven from persecution. Some may have left close relatives in precarious or unknown circumstances. Families of certain pupils may have travelled widely and the children will have rich and varied experiences of living in several countries. For others the journey to Britain may have been their first.

Some will come from rural and others from urban environments. The climate, food, clothing, transport, vegetation and housing they encounter here may be strange or relatively familiar. Some will have daunting family responsibilities, particularly if they become one of the more fluent English speakers in their household. Others will need to take on jobs in the home, family or business.

There is an increasing body of literature concerning the needs of refugees (e.g. Rutter, 1994). Despite the recent tightening up of immigration procedures, refugees, including unaccompanied children, continue to arrive in Britain and in our schools.

> Forced by persecution to leave their own countries, refugees often arrive in Britain traumatised and disorientated. Education, in particular language support, is often the route to self-sufficiency and a new life. (Refugee Council, undated)

Even well established communities have problems of acceptance and adjustment. Some members of the Vietnamese community, for example, even though they may have lived in London for twenty years still feel isolated and vulnerable. As Carty (1995) notes: 'Refugees are wary of seeking help and language presents a particular problem... In Vietnam once you've left school you don't go back.'

As well as having specific needs there is much that these pupils can contribute and much that we can learn from them. How we do this is a matter of sensitivity. Children should not be 'spotlighted' or assumed to represent their countries of origin. They might be greatly embarrassed by being asked direct and public questions or feeling pressured into revealing more about their experiences than they wish. Nor, in an attempt to make pupils feel welcomed, should teachers present themselves or their resources as experts on what others have experienced, by, for example 'doing' Bangladesh.

The solution, as in so many matters, is to provide opportunities for pupils to contribute as much or as little as they wish and feel ready for. There should always be space, without pressure, for pupils to speak or write about their background and feelings, to share or to remain private.

Racism is a common experience of the majority of bilingual pupils and their families. This can be personal, directed at individuals and take the form of verbal or physical abuse. Much racism is institutional, however and is the result of lack of awareness or provision within the social structures. The extent to which it is still acceptable for those in power to identify specific ethnic groups with 'social problems', the lack of provision for ethnic minorities within, say sheltered housing, the inappropriacy of health services, the lack of career opportunities for Black youth are common forms of discrimination which pupils and their families experience on a regular basis. To ignore these realities in our schools and classrooms would be to deny pupils part of their existence.

The concept of *culture* is also problematic. The term is widely used in often undefined senses. It can be used to refer to a range of norms and customs which are part of a society and include history, language, literature, religion and other social aspects of life. One sometimes sees language mentioned as separate from culture and in other cases culture seems to mean those exotic aspects of 'other cultures' which include food, clothing, traditional dances, festivals etc. It is a useful experience for each of us to try to define our own culture, rather than that of others.

Culture is a useful term but must be understood as dynamic, complex and flexible. It cannot be represented simply by an African fabric, an Indian sitar or a dish of rice and peas. It can be damaging if it is used to define and categorise people or to stereotype them and expectations of them. We must remain aware that cultures change and that part of that change is driven by new experiences and encounters. All pupils come to school with cultural as well as personal experiences and there is a two-way relationship between culture and learning in the school environment.

> '...a culture is constantly in process of being recreated as it is interpreted and renegotiated by its members. In this view, a culture is as much a *forum* for negotiating and re-negotiating meaning and for explicating action as it is a set of rules or specifications for action' (Bruner, 1986, original emphasis).

One of the things we need to establish at an early stage is the pupil's religion. Care must be taken not to make assumptions based on the declared religion. Beliefs and practices may vary and within many religions there are orthodox and liberal views. The extent to which particular rituals are followed and the importance attached to them depends on the individual. But religious observance can affect not only attendance at assembly and RE but also other aspects of school life such as dietary requirements. Some pupils may need to have a room set aside for prayer or contemplation. Attendance at particular times of the day, week or year may be affected. These matters will need to be clearly established at admission and the necessary adjustments made.

Ethnicity is sometimes confused with nationality. Anecdotes about pairing pupils who share the same language when in fact they come from politically opposed communities or nations, are still too prevalent.

Other less easily defined aspects of culture will also influence behaviour. The norms for polite behaviour in one society could be very different from those in another and so be open to misinterpretation. Parents, who may or may not have direct experience of the education system, can have different expectations, too. In one society it may be usual for parents to leave all educational matters to the professionals, whereas in another they might expect a high degree of involvement and consultation.

The opportunities for misunderstanding are a legion and it is not always possible to anticipate when they will occur. It requires patient explanation and open-mindedness on the part of schools and teachers as representatives of powerful institutions in order to minimise the difficulties. It also requires a willingness on the part of all to listen, learn, admit mistakes and make changes where necessary.

Responding to language diversity

One of the most important aspects of culture that bilinguals bring to our schools and classrooms is their *bilingualism*. The changing attitudes towards pupils' first languages and the more positive approach evident in some of the documentation have been referred to earlier. Teachers are now more aware that pupils are already fluent users of at least one, and in many cases several, languages. Bilingualism is widespread and many children will have grown up with some command of several languages, often including English. Children from the Indian sub-continent for example, may speak the official national, the state and the local language, use a different language for religious purposes and watch American videos and television films. Even after a short time in

Britain children can hardly fail to have some awareness of English, in both written and spoken form. This contributes to their overall knowledge about language which is often highly sophisticated.

There is a growing body of research which indicates the benefits of bilingualism in terms of children's metalinguistic awareness. Since bilinguals operate on and in the world in at least two languages it might be expected that they have a greater awareness of language as a system. Talking to bilingual children gives an insight into their understanding of the different and appropriate use of their languages. Blackledge (1994) quotes Saima (Yr 6) who says;

> In school it depends who I am talking to, like to the teachers or to Emma I will talk in English and to Saiqa I will talk in English because she usually talks in English but to Noreen or Shazma I will talk in both languages because they usually talk in both languages. When I am talking about maths, I will say half sentences in Mirpuri and half in English, or I will say half a paragraph in each language. (p.54)

What is interesting is not only Saima's awareness of her changing language use but also her command of the terms with which to describe it.

A Pakistani woman quoted by Miller (1983) shows similar explicitness:

> Whether I would prefer to express myself in Urdu, Punjabi or English depends really on who I'm talking to. If I'm talking to my Pakistani friends then I would quite happily switch over to Punjabi, because it's a bit more expressive, and a bit more ruthless. Urdu is a bit poetic and a somewhat aristocratic language. (p.48)

It is also clear to these people that some things are easier to express in one language and one context than another. Typically, aspects of schooling that are most closely associated with home, such as cooking, shopping, relationships, housing etc. are more readily expressed in first language.

It also seems that bilingual learners develop an understanding of the arbitrary nature of language earlier than do monolinguals. They realise that the word we choose to use for a particular object or idea is symbolic and does not attach to it. Because the four-legged animal that barks and wags its tail is called 'a dog' does not mean that it cannot also be 'ein Hund'. Cummins and Swain (1986) report on research to ascertain whether or not bilinguals have a greater appreciation of this arbitrary nature of language than monolinguals.

They conclude that bilingual children do indeed show a 'greater awareness of the arbitrary nature of word-referent relationships' (p.31).

This awareness is evident even in quite young children, as Gregory and Kelly (1994) report. Two Reception children are reading together when one of them demonstrates how well she can count in Bengali. The teacher, misunderstanding 'dosh' (ten) for 'gosh' comments, to which the child replies 'Mnn. But this is ten, dosh, not like gosh in 'Oh, my gosh, my golly.'' (p.198)

Other evidence suggests that bilinguals have a greater language learning readiness and facility than monolinguals. The experience of learning two language makes them more confident and better equipped to learn more about language. Teachers need to capitalise on these considerable existing abilities rather than problematise the relative lack of fluency in English.

Finally, it is important to recognise bilingual learners' existing *cognitive and conceptual abilities*. Some children will have attended school in their country of origin. The education they received may have been traditional, often based on a British model and possibly leading to examinations such as 'O' levels. They may have attended a local school with large classes and little equipment, or a prestigious, fee-paying, well-resourced establishment Some schools will have placed great emphasis on literacy and literature, sometimes including English literature. Some children may not yet have learnt to read or write in any language although they will almost certainly have encountered print and have some understanding of its form and function.

Savva (1990) describes how one Bangladeshi boy was asked to do simple computations in Maths because his teacher based her assumptions about his educational ability on his lack of fluency in English. He finally became thoroughly exasperated and showed the teacher that in Bangladesh he had done far more complicated maths.

We also need to be aware of role of complementary education in which many children are participating in this country. Children may go to Saturday schools, Mosque school or supplementary schools to learn language, religious instruction or history and literature. They may also learn traditional school subjects such as maths and science. Although the methods and syllabuses may differ from those of the mainstream, the experiences and education that the children receive is no less valid and should be recognised. Children and their families and communities demonstrate enormous commitment in the amount of time and effort that they devote to this aspect of education.

Even if children have had no formal schooling before arriving in Britain they will have had many opportunities for learning. They may well have had responsibilities beyond the experience of many of their British contemporaries and have knowledge of commerce, food production, machinery and travel which contribute to their maturity and understanding. All these should be valued and incorporated into our reception of the whole child.

What bilingual learners need

It is becoming increasingly clear from the research that, far from hindering learning and language development, the use of the first language enhances achievement. As has been discussed in chapter 3, teachers need to recognise the value of first language maintenance and seek to sustain and develop it.

This raises the vexed question of first language assessment. It has a number of dimensions. On one level we are concerned with the extent of fluency in the first language. There is no evidence to suggest that children who have used a language other than English in their early years develop fluency any later than those who have been brought up using English. We must not make unwarranted assumptions about first language fluency on the basis of difficulties that pupils are experiencing in school, whether these be lack of fluency in English or other problems that their education presents them with. Romaine (1984), in her extensive research into bilingualism in several different countries, finds no evidence to suggest that language acquisition is a cognitive problem. She does agree that it can be an educational problem in as far as schools often lack understanding of the needs of bilingual learners.

There may be cases, particularly among older children who have operated in English for several years, of a growing preference for English and a lack of literacy skills in the language of the home and of parents. It is certainly the case, as the majority of bilingual teachers testify, that there are some topics that are easier to discuss in one language than another and what has been learnt in English may be more easily described in English. This may exacerbate the distance between home and school and add weight to assumptions about lack of fluency.

These cases only confirm the need for priority and value to be given to first language within the school. Judging cognitive achievement through the first language is another aspect of assessment that requires careful consideration. Unless pupils feel able to show what they know and understand through their preferred language, or through non-linguistic methods, their conceptual development will inevitably be misjudged.

There is no doubt that bilingual learners also have an urgent need to develop English language skills in both oracy and literacy. We do them a disservice if we do not provide the support necessary to achieve fluency.

It has been clear for many years, although it is still not always firmly established within the education system, that language development and learning must go on side by side. Arguments about withdrawal have been rehearsed many times and the evidence supports the benefits of 'mainstreaming'. These benefits are of three types.

In educational terms it is vital that cognitive development is not delayed while 'language catches up'. Bilingual learners have a right to continue their learning and this is most effectively done in mainstream classrooms where teachers are familiar with the curriculum and with the most effective ways of making it accessible (Wiles, 1985). Teachers sometimes take the view that although this is feasible in the early years, when literacy skills are being developed and practical activities constitute a considerable element of learning it is less easy at secondary level. However, 'An important key to successful second language acquisition and academic achievement by adolescents may be uninterrupted academic instruction during the acquisition of basic L2 skills' (Collier, 1989).

Linguistically there are advantages in developing a new language in the company of those who speak and use it in normal settings and for a range of purposes. Peer models are generally more powerful than adults and the only way in which a natural language environment is attainable in school is in the classroom, playground, dinner queue and tutor group.

There are also powerful social arguments against withdrawal. It is sometimes claimed that young children in particular enjoy the 'special feeling' of being taken away from the classroom. If removing small groups is normal practice and those groups are mixed in ability, race and gender and are being taken out to, say, cook or tape-record, then this is not special, but normal. If, however, groups of bilingual learners, many of whom will also be black, are removed on a regular basis it can be seen by them and others as divisive and racist. They can also equate it with Special Needs withdrawal. The comfort that some children seem to derive from a place of security in a withdrawal group should lead us to question the relative insecurity of the classroom environment from which they have come and how this might be improved.

Children have learning as well as linguistic needs, and must not be allowed to stagnate in their conceptual development. There is an obligation on all teachers to continue to support the learning development of bilinguals as well as other pupils. Learning cannot wait upon language development.

Bilingual learners have personal and social needs which schools must consider and fulfil. School serves a powerful social and socialising function. It is here that pupils will develop the values of respect, collaboration, achievement and justice that are part of every home and community. They will also learn to balance the conflicts that arise and to cope with the problems as well as the strengths that human relationships bring.

Meeting the need – the first few weeks

Children who are new to a school or classroom need to be greeted and welcomed in ways that makes them feel secure and included. This is true for all children, whatever their language and background. Teachers should not feel dismayed at the arrival of pupils with very limited English. Bilingual learners may need additional support; they do not need radically different treatment.

Much of the preparation for new arrivals should be made in advance. If a school has a positive attitude to bilingualism and a welcoming ethos then much of this preparation will be in place. Language and admissions policies will be relevant and need to be referred to. The policies themselves should be regularly reviewed, discussed and monitored. Local authority policies on housing and placement and the support of new arrivals and refugees should also be consulted.

How has the authority decided on pupil placement? Are there other members of the family of school age? Where are they placed? What provision is made for social, housing, health and benefits advice and support? Where are records held? Is information shared? Are funds available for extra support to the school? Is there information about agencies which might offer advice?

In terms of school policy and practice many supportive aspects may already be in place. For example there may be information booklets and reports in a number of community languages. The curriculum may include issues of migration, countries of origin and non-European languages and literature, supported with suitable resources. Policies about the importance of first language and how to support it, and about the deployment and responsibilities of teaching and non-teaching staff in this area, may already be in place together with strategies for parental involvement and how to extend it. There may already be an ESL department or LEA support team. Strong links may already exist with the local community.

Staff may welcome information about the language and community from which their pupils come, including the correct name for the language – Twi, not African, Urdu not Pakistani. It should be possible to find out something about the script and language varieties and basic structures and to learn a few phrases in the language. Local Section 11 teams will have accumulated information on the major languages spoken in the area. They may have literature about them and materials written in those languages . There should also be a list of agencies which can give additional advice and support. Teachers are not counsellors and although the pastoral role is of great importance they need to know when and where to obtain specialist advice. Organisations such as the Refugee Council, the CRE, Runnymede Trust and the local authority can give lists of appropriate contacts.

The extent to which good practices are firmly embedded within the school, whether or not policies exist, will be crucial in helping new arrivals to settle. The flexibility and appropriacy of admissions policies will also need to be considered, particularly if pupils arrive during the school year. School secretaries are often the first contact that parents or carers have with the school and it is important that a welcoming and positive approach is adopted from the start. This means that non-teaching staff need to be fully involved in policy development and implementation.

Communication with parents is a two-way process. It will be extremely useful if the school can collect information about the pupil's background, previous experience and abilities on admission. There needs to be an accurate record of the child's names, religion, previous schooling and special requirements and of relevant information about parental languages. All this should be recorded as standard for all children in the school. The age of new arrivals is not always easy to establish. Birth certificates are not always available, nor is registration compulsory in all countries. In some cases the method of counting a person's age differs from the European, with a baby being counted as one year old in its first year of life.

It is also be useful to record aspects of community links, such as the appropriate language for communication with the home. It is important that superfluous information is not demanded. For example, recording the date of arrival or length of residence in the U.K has now been abandoned by some schools and authorities as being potentially threatening to some families.

The initial meeting or interview is also an opportunity to make introductions that will be of importance in the future. It may be helpful if an interpreter is available. Parents can be invited to come with a friend if their own English is weak. Interpreting is a delicate matter and strangers who speak a different dialect or are of a different class or religion from the visitors could raise rather than reduce barriers. Community advice should ideally be sought and this will depend on links already being in place.

Children themselves can find the initial meeting at the school intimidating. However, it does provide an opportunity to meet one or two classmates and the classteacher so that newcomers find a familiar face when they start. Even older children will be reassured by the presence of a parent, carer or sibling at the introductory stages. Much will depend on the friendliness and welcome of everyone connected with the school. A smile, a few words of greeting and a brief tour of the premises with relevant introductions will leave a good and lasting impression.

Parents will want information about the school and possibly about the education system in general. Some will have had very different experiences of education themselves and be unfamiliar with the National Curriculum, progress through the Years, testing and the regulations for uniform, attendance and public examinations. A simple booklet outlining the statutory requirements and the way in which the school meets them will be a useful source of information. This should ideally be translated into the main community languages. Schools are increasingly producing such booklets, illustrated with photographs and children's work. Some schools have experimented with introductory videos, often made by pupils and some have 'voice-overs' in various languages. These can be lent to families. Photographs with the names of staff can be displayed in the entrance lobby of the school as a useful introduction and reminder for new parents.

Decisions about placing a pupil will also have to be made. In some circumstances there will be little or no choice, but there are a number of considerations and personnel who should be involved. It will be relevant to look at the distribution of other bilingual pupils in the school. If possible new arrivals should be placed in a class or tutor group with others who share their first language. The availability of language support will also need to be considered and the experience of those teachers with whom they will have most contact is also of significance. There may be a question of which option choices or bands, sets or streams the pupils should be placed in. As far as possible these decisions need to be flexible and made in consultation with those who know the pupil and his/her needs. It should certainly not be assumed that if English is new to pupils they should automatically be placed in the lowest set or stream or that only non-academic options are suitable. Some subjects are more linguistically demanding than others, particularly those that are relatively abstract or rely heavily on a knowledge of English history or literature. But it should not be assumed that these subjects are beyond the cognitive capabilities of pupils, even if the linguistic demands need considerable support at the early stages.

Preparing for a new pupil

The number of staff, teaching and non-teaching, who need to be given information and involved in decisions about new arrivals will differ in primary and secondary schools. Heads of Year will typically liaise with both pastoral and academic staff, but cases of pupils suddenly appearing in the class of a teacher who has had no advance information are not unknown and are irritating for the teacher and distressing for the pupil. Communication is a vital aspect of every institution and schools will need to evaluate their own procedures. 'Need to know' policies may have to be reviewed.

Once a suitable class or tutor group has been identified they can be prepared to a certain extent before the new member arrives. If classmates are expecting their new colleague and have discussed how to welcome him/her, the first few days are likely to be more successful for all concerned. Pupils will have memories of their own first days and be able to empathise and make suggestions about problems and solutions. It is helpful to discuss language matters with pupils and to think about some of the difficulties a new arrival could face and how to overcome them. It may be possible to learn a few words of greeting in the pupil's language.

Both the 'buddy' system and peer tutoring have been found to be supportive to new pupils. It helps to choose a buddy, or buddies, if they share a language. But even if this is not possible giving pupils the responsibility of helping and introducing a new classmate can be a positive experience for all. Thought will have to be given to pupils who are likely to be suitable 'buddies' and several children might share the responsibility. Their duties and how to meet them should be discussed. Certain times of the day such as arrival and departure, playtime/breaks and lunch, which are often less structured, can be stressful. It will be relevant to discuss bullying, harassment and racism and how to deal with them and to involve non-teaching staff who have supervisory responsibilities.

Peer tutoring has been found to be supportive of both tutor and tutee if there has been sufficient preparation (Curtis, 1992). It involves identifying a pupil who shares the same first language as the newcomer and who can take responsibility for translating and supporting in lessons. It is important to discuss with the pupil what her/his role could be and what will be most helpful to the newcomer. Curtis found that established pupils often welcomed the opportunity to clarify their own understandings and to take on a 'teacherly' role and that this helped the new arrivals to engage more fully with the learning.

The first days

Even with the best preparation certain issues cannot be anticipated or resolved until the pupil actually arrives. Strategies need to be in place to deal with any problems as soon as possible. It help to designate one person, often the class or form teacher, or alternatively the ESL post-holder, as the person with ultimate responsibility, to whom the pupil knows s/he can turn when necessary. This requires that person to be available and accessible when needed, which is not always easy in the life of a school. A compromise might be to set aside a certain time and place each day when individual and sole attention is given to the new arrival.

Any new pupil will find the first few days difficult until they adjust to the new people and lay-out of the school. There are many inexplicit rules of behaviour and communication that we are only vaguely aware of and that are learnt over time through observation and copying. Bilingual learners will need a period of adjustment and may cope by having an extended silent period, during which they are learning and listening a great deal, although they may not yet be ready for active, oral participation. We also need to be aware of the concentration required and frustration that may be felt by someone who is operating for a long time in an unfamiliar language and environment. Young children may fall asleep, older ones may show their distress through withdrawn or aggressive behaviour. These reactions must be treated with understanding, not punishment.

The new arrival has learning and linguistic needs which cannot be 'put on hold', although it may be some time before they appear to become involved in lessons.

Some schools provide a booklet or tape of 'survival' vocabulary for the pupil in English and their first language. If the pupil is pre-literate a series of drawings or symbols may help them to request the toilet, know the time or choose an activity by pointing to the appropriate picture. Signs and labels can be provided in a number of scripts. The classroom will then seem more familiar, and literate pupils will be provided with immediate guidance.

Staff should make a point of addressing new pupils directly, with appropriate gestures and action, and involving them in the life of the classroom. They should not expect or demand a verbal response but involve pupils in giving out equipment, lining up quietly or arranging the books. The pupil should be spoken to in normal language, not 'broken' or 'pidgin' English and using natural repetition. Time taken by teachers to learn a few phrases of the pupil's first language will be well spent. It will take time for the learner to sort out some of the English, but the repetition of routines will be extremely helpful. Some of their earliest learning will be whole phrases in English, such as 'line-up-quietly,' or 'get-out-your-reading-books' which they may well imitate. Many phrases will be learnt from peers, some undoubtedly picked up in the playground, and including expletives or swear words. Aggression or ostracisation needs to be dealt with immediately, and here non-teaching staff and older children can help.

Some support for language development may be available from other adults. Trained ESL and bilingual teachers have an important role to play, not only directly with the pupil, but also by giving advice to teachers. Parents, siblings and other members of the community should be encouraged to work with groups of children that include new arrivals. Small group work can provide a secure environment for both learning and, where possible, first language use. Use of the first language, both oral and literate, should be encouraged on every occasion involving pupils and other members of the pupil's language community. Monolingual teachers need not feel threatened by their inability to understand what is being said or written. Some discourse will be translated at the time or later. Teachers do not need to overhear or partici-pate in everything that is being discussed, in English or any other language.

An important role of teachers and other adults will be to observe the child's attitude and participation in activities in the classroom and playground. Formal assessment is not appropriate or accurate at this stage but a record of language and learning, with supporting evidence, can be started almost immediately. Section 11 teachers or others will make broad judgements about the learner's stage of English fluency, but this should be regarded as tentative, at least until the child shows evidence of having settled and gained in confidence. Certainly, any assessment of Special Educational Need should not be contemplated yet.

Language and learning take place simultaneously so pupils need and want to be involved in classroom activities right from the start. Children are realists and they know that not all the learning will be accessible to them at an early stage, but neither do they deserve to be 'fobbed off' with mindless colouring or copying tasks.

Practical activities and those involving non-linguistic communication are most readily accessible. Pictures, charts and diagrams can be used to support learning. Resources should be available in several languages and listening activities can include tapes which can be replayed for reinforcement. It may be possible for bilingual staff or parents to make tapes to support particular lessons or tasks, for example, a set of instructions in science, or a synopsis of the text to be read in an English lesson.

Learners will gain most from being part of collaborative activities which involve natural and sometimes repeated language. In these groups they may have the opportunity to use their first language to ask questions and receive answers. They should in any case have the support of peers who will repeat, demonstrate and explain, as far as they are able, the task and the learning.

All teachers must see themselves as being simultaneously subject and language teachers. They should make time to help their bilingual pupils to summarise and reflect on what they have learnt. In the early days this will probably need to be orally in the first language and with a bilingual speaker, whether a teacher, helper, parent or pupil. Before very long, pupils will be able to write brief summaries in English or the first language (McGahern, 1994).

Supportive materials

Developing bilinguals need appropriate resources to support their language and learning. It is important that these are relevant to the cognitive and interest level of the children as well as to their linguistic level. This can present a difficulty for older pupils, although an increasing number of resources are being produced, both nationally and locally, for this age group. Games and picture books are relatively accessible for all young children, whatever their language skills, but would be demeaning for older learners. Increasingly, books and other resources in languages other than English are being imported and, even if printed in monochrome on poor quality paper, can provide a valuable method of presenting concepts and of valuing previous learning when they are used alongside other resources.

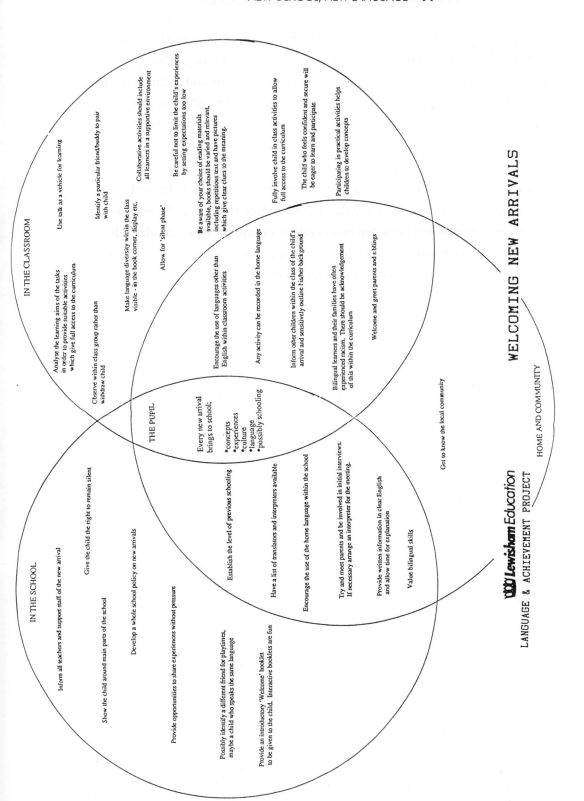

IN THE CLASSROOM

Use talk as a vehicle for learning

Collaborative activities should include all learners in a supportive environment

Identify a particular friend/buddy to pair with child

Be careful not to limit the child's experiences by setting expectations too low

Analyse the learning aims of the tasks in order to provide suitable activities which give full access to the curriculum

Make language diversity within the class visible - in the book corner, display etc.

Be aware of your choice of reading materials available, books should be varied and relevant, including repetitious text and have pictures which give clear clues to the meaning.

Observe within class group rather than withdraw child

Allow for 'silent phase'

Fully involve child in class activities to allow full access to the curriculum

The child who feels confident and secure will be eager to learn and participate

Encourage the use of languages other than English within classroom activities

Participating in practical activities helps children to develop concepts

Any activity can be recorded in the home language

Inform other children within the class of the child's arrival and sensitively outline his/her background

THE PUPIL

Every new arrival brings to school;

*concepts
*experiences
*culture
*language
*possibly schooling

Bilingual learners and their families have often experienced racism. There should be acknowledgement of this within the curriculum

Welcome and greet parents and siblings

IN THE SCHOOL

Inform all teachers and support staff of the new arrival

Give the child the right to remain silent

Show the child around main parts of the school

Develop a whole school policy on new arrivals

Provide opportunities to share experiences without pressure

Establish the level of previous schooling

Possibly identify a different friend for playtimes, maybe a child who speaks the same language

Have a list of translators and interpreters available

Provide an introductory "Welcome' booklet to be given to the child. Interactive booklets are fun

Encourage the use of the home language within the school

Try and meet parents and be involved in initial interviews. If necessary arrange an interpreter for the meeting.

Provide written information in clear English and allow time for explanation

Value bilingual skills

Get to know the local community

WELCOMING NEW ARRIVALS

HOME AND COMMUNITY

Lewisham Education

LANGUAGE & ACHIEVEMENT PROJECT

Teachers will produce many materials themselves and these need to enable developing bilinguals to have access to the learning even though their understanding of English is still limited. Charts, diagrams, maps and pictures with clear and direct language all support understanding. The abilities and experiences of all pupils should be taken into account and the resources should be relevant to them.

All teachers have a responsibility to meet the needs of all their pupils, whether these be cognitive or linguistic. Ultimately we can be reassured that good teaching is good teaching and that teachers who learn from the achievements of their pupils will be in the best position to support new arrivals. 'The extra dimension that makes it work for bilingual pupils is a sensitivity to what it is like to be a language learner in the classroom' (Edwards, 1995).

Chapter 5

A Relevant Curriculum

The National Curriculum has provided a framework of what pupils should be able to 'know, understand and do' at key points in their learning. It seems to have removed from teachers the responsibility, which was never entirely theirs anyway, of deciding curriculum content. However we still have to decide, within this broad outline, how to make the learning accessible and relevant to all our pupils and what to do if, despite our best efforts, some still appear to fail. Reports continue to indicate that ethnic minority pupils under-achieve in disproportionate numbers (see Klein, 1993, Gillborn, 1995).

There could be a number of reasons for their failure. Arguments have been put forward for inherent lack of ability, for example the right-wing academics and educationalists who continue to suggest that black children have low IQs, or are in some other way deficient. Or alternatively, family patterns and socialisation are blamed.

Another view is that the curriculum has limited relevance to ethnic minority pupils and that a motivating and interesting syllabus will lead to greater achievement. Others argue that changes need to be made in the approach to teaching and learning and that classroom organisation and ethos is the key factor.

Alternatively, the explanation might be found in the assessment criteria themselves. It could be that we are using inappropriate measures of achievement and that using different criteria and recognising other attainments and successes would produce a different picture.

Solutions, then, should be sought in the learners, the curriculum, teaching methods and materials or in the ways of assessing success.

Learners

One way of characterising changing attitudes to ethnic minority communities is in terms of the prevailing political beliefs and assumptions. Mullard (1982) suggests that the 1950s and 60s were a period of assimilationism within education. There was the expectation and hope that black pupils would become so much part of society and its shared values that they would in effect 'disappear'. Mullard argues that this approach was founded on assumptions of national unity and a definable British culture – white, Anglo-Saxon, protestant – in which everyone participated and with which they all identified. 'Immigrants', it was argued, had chosen to come to Britain partly to become part of this culture and therefore 'they' should adapt and become 'one of us'. For this to take place the best approach on the part of schools and teachers was to be 'colour blind' and not treat black pupils in any way differently from white. 'They' would change and become absorbed and if 'they' did not do so voluntarily then they would have to be persuaded.

The persuasion took the form of compensatory education programmes which were designed to make up for the unfortunate but inevitable deficits that 'they' brought with them. Evidence for this assumed lack of ability, or perhaps intelligence, was provided by tests which confirmed the inadequacy of previous education.

In the mid-1960s this view was modified from the assimilationist to an integrationist model. It was conceded that assimilation seemed to have failed and was recognised that minorities also had rights. Roy Jenkins, then Home Secretary, in a speech in 1966 described integration as: 'not the flattening process of assimilation but an equal opportunity accompanied by cultural diversity in an atmosphere of mutual tolerance' (quoted in Sarup, 1986)

So even if black culture and language caused 'problems', the search for equality demanded that it be tolerated. Low achievement was attributed to poor self-image. Accordingly some schools introduced Black Studies programmes, for black youngsters to learn more about 'their' heroes, history and music and so enhance their 'self-image'. These views did not, however, permeate the high status, academic curriculum. Stone (1981) was fierce a critic of the attitude underlying these programmes, which she saw as misguided and patronising. Stone demanded that black children be given the same educational opportunities as their white counterparts.

The school system has never reflected the culture of the majority of children in the country who are working class. Why then this concern to reflect the culture of small sections of that class – West Indian and other minority group children? (Stone, quoted in Sarup, 1986)

Underachievement, however, continued and the cause, and therefore the remedy, was diagnosed as lying with the learners, their families and communities. One of the educational responses was to concentrate resources, time and materials on remediating the individual and differentiating the curriculum. ESL teachers worked largely with individuals or small groups of pupils to teach them English, while special needs groups were disproportionately weighted with African-Caribbean pupils.

Hart (1986) discusses some of the underlying assumptions in the special needs approach to remediation and which apply equally to ethnic minority pupils. If individual children are seen as having difficulties then the issue for the teacher is to investigate the nature of these and provide appropriate materials and support. Such children are immediately identified as 'having something wrong' and being in need of special and often individual provision. Teachers were required to spend time diagnosing need and producing special materials or using different techniques, in order to compensate for the perceived deficit in the pupil.

The arguments for differentiation being put forward today are somewhat similar and are also based on the diagnosis of individual differences. Differentiation is seen as a process of intervention based on individual needs in order to maximise pupils' potential. It is usually presented in terms of equality of opportunity. Pupils, it is argued, respond to a variety of teaching styles and use different learning strategies so materials and forms of classroom organisation have to be adapted to meet these needs.

Critics of this approach have argued that equality of opportunity is not possible in a society which perpetuates inequality through its institutions and practices and that to attempt to enhance individual access while retaining discriminatory procedures is to avoid the real issue. We need to re-evaluate and make changes in the curriculum, in our pedagogy and in our means of assessment rather than problematise learners who underachieve in an unequal system. Cummins, an advocate of first language development in raising the achievement of bilingual learners, nevertheless states:

The crucial element in reversing language minority students' school failure is not the language of instruction but the extent to which educators work to reverse – rather than perpetuate – the subtle, and often not so subtle, institutionalised racism of the society as a whole (Cummins, 1986, original emphasis).

Debates which focus on the learners tend to see them as passive recipients of knowledge transmitted by the teacher. This view ignores or underestimates the part pupils play in their own learning and concentrates instead on the role of the teacher as provider of information.

Curriculum content

Child-centred education has been invoked to support the view of learning which places the learner at the heart of education. It derives from the work of Piaget, who saw learners as creators of their own understanding. Their view of the world is constructed, he argued, from their interaction with it. Piaget was not an educationalist and did not offer suggestions about teaching method but others extrapolated from his argument that the teacher's role was to provide a stimulating environment within which the child could experiment and learn about her/his environment. This was certainly the approach of the Plowden Report (1967).

Importantly in terms of arguments about curriculum content, Piaget saw child development as a series of stages, of which the earliest were to do with physical control. The ability to 'decentre' or take the viewpoint of others developed relatively late, when the child was six or seven, suggesting that, at least in the early years, the curriculum should be entirely concerned with basic skills and that activities or discussions touching on issues of inequality, sexism or racism, would be ineffective. Yet there is significant evidence of young children thinking and talking about what is fair and unfair. Epstein (1993), for example, describes how well nursery children reflected on boys' and girls' access to and use of building bricks and wheeled toys.

Psychologists such as Donaldson (1978) and Wood (1988) have challenged the notion of the ego-centric child and the arbitrary nature of Piaget's stages of development. Whereas Piaget saw children as individuals interacting with their environment, Bruner and Vygotsky have stressed the social nature of learning. Children learn, they suggest, by being 'tutored' by more experienced people who provide the support necessary for them to achieve a little more than they can presently do alone. As skills and understanding in one area develop, that support or 'scaffold', can gradually be removed and transferred to a different activity. Learning is therefore based on transactions, shared understanding and rule making. It requires some areas of joint reference between the learner and the tutor who then work to overcome ambiguities. Formal education is one of the most important means by which this takes place.

These joint understandings are part of what we mean by culture. Education, then, is as much about induction into 'common knowledge' as it is about the acquisition of information and skills. But if the learning process is a collaborative one, in which the learner forms the rules and disentangles the ambiguities with the help of others, it must also be a creative process. To make knowledge one's own requires a basis from which to develop, extend and re-organise. If learning were simply a matter of transmitting information from the knowledgeable to the ignorant there would be no possibility of change or development. Learners create new juxtapositions, new solutions and new questions. They do this through interaction.

> Learning ... is a communal activity, a sharing of the culture. It is not just that the child must make his (sic) knowledge his own, but that he must make it his own in a community of those who share his sense of belonging to a culture. (Bruner, 1986,p.127)

This suggests that a vital aspect of the learning environment is the cultural assumptions and shared experiences that underpin it. Some of the thinking that lies behind a cultural pluralist or multicultural approach to education is informed by the constructivist view of learning. Integrationist practice had proved largely ineffective and was resented by many members of minority communities. Stone (1981) was particularly critical of the divisive nature of policies which seemed to affirm majority views of difference and inferiority. Carby (1982) saw equality of opportunity as an excuse to treat differences unequally and to re-locate the causes of black failure in individuals and their families.

Cultural pluralism, on the other hand, seemed to recognise and promote a positive view of diversity. All pupils, it was argued, should be given the opportunity to develop their own culture. All cultures were to be valued and therefore represented in the classroom. The Select Committee on Race Relations and Immigration, 1969 already advocated....

Specific teaching about the countries from which the immigrants in any particular town come. Here material direct from those countries can be displayed in the classroom by immigrant children. Children in primary schools in Hackney or Brixton, for example could be taught West Indian songs, or children in Wolverhampton be shown Indian art, jewellery and costumes. This would help bring the immigrant children into the life of the school (quoted in Carby, 1982)

Bullock (1975) in the well-known statement about children's language, and Swann (1985) both seemed to support multicultural education while recognising the wide range of different interpretations of the term.

All LEAs should declare their commitment to the principles of 'education for all'; to the development of a pluralist approach to the curriculum, and to countering the influence of racism. (DES, 1985, p770)

The Swann report commented on the lack of multicultural approaches in predominantly white schools. It put forward the view that it was as much the responsibility of such schools to promote education for all as of those with more ethnically mixed populations. Multiculturalism was seen as necessary for equality of opportunity.

This perspective, in one form or another, has been extremely influential and is still widely supported and practised in many British schools. Publishers, aware of a market for multicultural materials, advertise diversity and the representation of different ethnic groups in the teaching resources they sell. Teachers' books and manuals describe ways in which different cultures can be represented in the classroom. Theorists have backed these practices with research evidence.

Cummins lists as the first of his pedagogical principles that:

The educational and personal experiences students bring to schools constitute the foundation for all their future learning; schools should therefore attempt to amplify rather than replace these experiences. (Cummins, 1994 p.40)

He amplifies this largely in terms of recognition of first language skills but also refers to value of their culture in the broader sense.

The National Curriculum has been criticised for failing to acknowledge the multicultural nature of society and for perpetuating an elitist view of education. The 1988 Education Act specifically addresses the need to provide for the education and development of all pupils and contains in its first section a statement of intent:

The curriculum of a school satisfies the requirements of the Act if it is a balanced and broadly based curriculum which:

a) promotes the spiritual, moral, cultural, mental and physical development of pupils at the school and of society; and

b) prepares such pupils for the opportunities, responsibilities and experiences of adult life' (Education Reform Act, 1988)

The revised National Curriculum, in place, we are promised, for at least five years, is largely Eurocentric. British history predominates, particularly in Key Stages 1 and 2, although there is opportunity at Key Stage 2 to study a past, non-European society. Geography concentrates on skills and the local environment in the early years and introduces study of other countries largely through thematic study. The Science and Maths curriculum give every indication that SCAA considers these subjects to be 'culture-free' and equally applicable in any society. Even the non-statutory examples offer few suggestions of how to introduce a broader perspective. The English orders mention that pupils should : 'read, analyse and evaluate a wide range of texts, including literature from the English literary heritage and from other cultures and traditions' (DFE, 1995).

Other languages and dialects are mentioned in terms of the contribution they can make to an understanding of standard English.

However, teachers have in the past been and will continue to be ingenious in their interpretations and implementation of the statutory requirements and may well be able to take advantage of the reduction in obligatory content to broaden the curriculum. Ofsted inspections may support their efforts, although recent revisions to the Framework for Inspection giving less emphasis to issues of equality are a worrying development.

Reading materials which feature people from a range of different backgrounds are widely available and a number of checklists exist which help teachers to select those that are most suitable (see for example, Stinton 1979, Preiswerk 1980, Klein 1984, Twitchin 1988, Barrs and Thomas 1991).

Teachers are becoming more sensitive to the need to portray girls and black people in positive roles, both in text and in pictures. Texts with words which can have negative connotations, such as 'native', 'primitive' and 'savage', are no longer prevalent in schools and the multicultural nature of society is to some extent reflected in our reading material and textbooks.

From the earliest years of schooling children can read poetry, plays and stories from different cultures which 'include a range of narrative structures and literary techniques' and 'draw on oral and literary traditions'. More writing of this kind is being translated into English and attractively produced. The Key Stage 3 and 4 reading list, however, gives very few examples of literature from outside the UK and the recommendation to use 'poems of high quality by major writers with well established critical reputations' needs to be interpreted imaginatively. Opportunities also need to be created to include non-fiction and media texts which reflect the range of cultures in society.

The Programme of Study for Key Stage 1 Mathematics stipulates that pupils learn the language of maths and are able, for example, to compare size and shape. What they are to compare and discuss or sort and classify is not specified. Much stimulating work has been done using patterns from different cultures to 'develop ideas of regularity and sequencing'. Teachers describe using Islamic designs to develop ideas of symmetry and tessellation (see Shan and Bailey, 1991) Similarly the development and use of different number systems and methods of counting and recording are a feature of many primary maths topics.

In the secondary phase understanding and using functional relationships and the interpretation of graphs in maths can readily draw upon statistics on world poverty or comparative GNP to study and represent in various ways. Many of the theorems and techniques used in Western mathematics originate in China or the Arab world (see for example Ifrah, 1985) and this needs to be taught to pupils.

Science is another curriculum area which requires imagination to extend the Programmes of Study. At Key Stage 1 pupils have to 'relate their understanding of science to domestic and environmental contexts'. We can ensure that those contexts are sufficiently varied to represent a range of cultural experiences. Cooking utensils from many parts of the world can be used to illustrate heat retention and conduction; pictures of water conservation projects from Africa and Asia are relevant environmental contexts; food and nutrition can readily include global examples of agriculture and explore where our food comes from.

Key Stage 3 Science: Life Processes and Living Things, can provide the opportunity to investigate the concept of race itself, as well as diseases such as sickle cell anaemia which are specific to a particular group of people. In Physical Processes, work on the solar system can feature the contributions of astronomers from non-Western countries to our understanding of the universe.

Similar opportunities exist in the other curriculum areas to ensure that lifestyles and histories are reflected in a positive way in the classroom and a more inclusive view of world knowledge is promoted.

Pedagogy

A version of multicultural education which simply sets out to celebrate diversity has been widely criticised as ignoring the realities of pupils' lives and of the society in which we live. It tends to be tokenistic making a gesture towards recognition of other ways of life that is often superficial and patronising. Equality of opportunity cannot be achieved in an unequal society which denies minority groups access to decision-making and power. Multiculturalism can give the impression of meeting children's needs without changing actual levels of achievement. Celebrating Diwali while Hindu children continue to under-achieve in school is to place the problem with the pupils. Such multi-culturalism does no more than starting with the child's experiences and sharing them with others. If they are not put in a position from which to critically examine their learning then pupils are less able to challenge the social and political structures that reinforce their underachievement and permit racist practices to continue.

Equality of opportunity was used in the past as an argument for separate and special treatment. There was fear that it might now be used to argue for a sameness or averaging out, which could militate against quality. Critics of a cultural pluralist approach argued that recognising the social and political realities which deny equality was a crucial part of education and that if the curriculum incorporated opportunities not only to learn about one's own and other societies and cultures, but also to analyse and criticise them, then quality and equality need not be incompatible.

The report *Education for Some* (Eggleston, Dunn and Anjali, 1986) began by looking at post-compulsory education and the curriculum from the point of view of the participants – teachers and other professionals such as youth workers and students. The finding that, whatever the intention, students experienced education as racist in effect led to some recommendations in terms of curriculum provision. For example, students who have chosen to remain in education should be given more autonomy and choice in the range of options from which to select and these options should be vocational as well as academic.

Gillborn (1990) studied African-Caribbean boys in secondary education. His findings confirm the existence of racism in schools but reveal how different pupils respond differently. By confronting racist teachers and practices some pupils become increasingly alienated and are defined as deviant. They often 'fail' in educational terms. Others accommodate to avoid criticism and so are more likely to remain within the system and to be regarded as successes. Their achievement could be interpreted by educationalists as confirming the values of the traditional curriculum, although it may in fact be at the expense of a pupil's autonomy and identity.

A curriculum for equality is one which takes account of what pupils from different backgrounds are learning from it. It does not present 'other' cultures as exotic or 'interesting', but engages all learners in raising questions and moving towards different answers. It gives learners a voice.

In some ways the content of the curriculum for equality may look little different from an uncritical multicultural curriculum but the difference lies in the approach taken. Richardson (1990), drawing on the work of Freire, has characterised the main perspectives as conforming, reforming and transforming. A conforming view is approximately equivalent to the assimilationist and integrationist approaches, summarised by Richardson as 'when in Rome do as the Romans do'. Cultural pluralism which reforms the curriculum in order to celebrate diversity is based on individual rather than structural change. Transformation on the other hand, recognises the discriminatory structures in society that prevent justice and achievement for all In a transformed education there would be more black teachers and administrators in influential positions. Racism and its causes would become a subject of study, rather than simply a problem whose effects have to be dealt with.

If we are to be educational transformers one of the first questions we must ask concerns the nature of knowledge itself. The National Curriculum has a particular view and selection of knowledge based on the Western liberal tradition. Whatever the validity of that view it is only one of several. Just as there are different approaches to literacy, so there are different views of knowledge. Popper, for example, challenged the generally accepted notion of scientific knowledge as a set of observable facts by suggesting that science found the most convincing explanations for the way the world appeared to operate. These explanations could be and were challenged and overturned from time to time as new observations suggested different and better-fit explanations.

Knowledge is not culture-free. Western mathematics defines a triangle as a three-sided figure whose internal angles add up to 180 degrees and this is the geometrical knowledge that pupils learn. Many African cultures, however, have different mathematical descriptions and definitions and therefore different views of what constitutes a triangle (see Zaslavsky, 1973). Vedic mathematics, possibly the oldest in the world, offers formulations for solving mathematical problems which are very different from traditional Western ones (see Shan and Bailey, 1991).

Learning is about asking questions. Surveys continue to confirm the findings of the ORACLE project (see Galton, 1989), that most questioning is done by teachers rather than pupils. Most of these questions are not genuine in the sense of seeking to discover new information but are usually a form of assessment, to check what pupils have understood or remembered (see Edwards and Mercer 1987). Education for equality implies a change in pedagogy towards more pupil-generated questions. Collaborative learning is one way in which pupils can be given more control over their own learning, including formulating their own questions.

Learning resources

If we see knowledge as a social construct and one which involves the active participation of the learner, we must also allow for the selection and control of that knowledge to be shared by all. The National Curriculum may not give us much scope for this but it does allow us to make knowledge itself an issue. Books, for instance, are thought by many people to present truths which are not open to challenge but this apparent authority can be questioned. Even in the nursery, children can have the experience of being authors and producing books themselves. Authors can be invited to discuss their work and be questioned about its perspectives. Goodwin and Wellings (1991) describe the involvement of junior children in evaluating and rearranging the school library. The pupils were able to discuss stereotyping, omission and bias in order to make judgements about the books.

Photographs are another excellent way of raising issues of truth and reality. Photographers select their viewpoint carefully in order to present a particular version of what they see. Children can extend photographs by drawing what is outside or beyond them. Or the photographs can be built up like jigsaws to give wider and wider views which change as they are added to.

A group of Yr 7 students in one Science lesson brainstormed the names of all the scientists they could think of. Groups spent a relatively short time in the library finding out about some of them and adding to the list This information was collated with the whole class to determine how many of the scientist were living and how many dead, who were male and female and who black or white. The findings provided the basis for asking questions about why pupils learn mainly about white, dead, male scientists.

Learners have their own knowledge and information and this must be given space in the classroom. It is not only teachers who select what is important. Docherty (1991) describes a topic on farming which empowered children to describe growing bananas in Guyana and make comparisons between Indian and Irish goat keeping. Docherty observes that: 'Each contribution was first hand knowledge capable of widening our understanding about farming in contemporary settings around the world' (p.11).

An area of knowledge that is particular to black students is the experience of racism. Other oppressed and powerless groups can begin to have an empathetic understanding of the experience, but black students remain the experts. It must be given space and investigated. There have been debates about the role of the white teacher in such discussions. Stenhouse (1982) and Jeffcoate (1984) are among those who advocate a neutral chair in order to permit all views to be expressed without pupils fearing the teacher's reaction. This approach has been criticised by Epstein (1993) and others as being dishonest and allowing the perpetuation of existing power structures. Teachers must make it clear where they stand on racism and handle any discussion in a sensitive way. Teachers' behaviour betrays their own positions, a fact which pupils quickly realise, so that to lay claim to neutrality is absurd. The Runnymede Trust (1993) provides a useful set of guidelines for teachers faced with controversial questions.

Discussions about racism can be subtle and thoughtful and might start from a poem or novel as well as directly from an incident. But black pupils should not be made to feel responsible for defending themselves or for having to make the anti-racist case, and their right to remain silent must be respected.

'Salt on a Snake's Tail', a short story by Farrukh Dhondy (1978) is set in the East End of London. It features a Bangladeshi family, so seemed a particularly suitable choice for the Yr 10 class in the secondary school in which I was working. There is also a video to help those bilingual pupils whose English was not yet fluent. However, I felt uneasy about the portrayal of some of the characters, in particular the father, who avoids trouble and confrontation and seems not just submissive but sly, and of the women characters who have passive and servile roles. The video portrays the East End as run-down and anarchic. I showed the video to the Bangladeshi pupils and discussed with them whether to use it with the whole Year 10 group. They agreed it was negative and we decided to work with a group of white students to make a video which gave a more realistic view of their area and to present a more sympathetic view of the father.

We read the story as a class. Pupils then had a number of statements to sort according to or not they agreed with them. They placed the statements on a grid which included quotes from the text and headings which highlighted aspects of the personalities involved. The video and alternative version were shown. Finally small groups of pupils worked on role-plays around some of the incidents in the story and then wrote them in the form of short stories. The activities gave rise to animated discussions about racism, both in the groups and the class as a whole, and allowed the black students to relate personal incidents or if they preferred, simply to discuss the issues purely in terms of the novel.

Younger children are also able to deal with controversial issues. Epstein (1993) describes an oral history project in which pupils interviewed their families to find out how long they had lived in the area, where they had come from and what they felt about the changes in the community and in their own lives. She points out that the children themselves raised questions about the racism that they and their families had experienced.

Many primary schools involve pupils in making surveys of how children use the playground and conducting interviews about how things might be changed. Issues of race and gender are often raised by these surveys and some of the most imaginative and practical solutions are suggested by the pupils themselves.

Occasions will arise, possibly in PHSE, RE or in response to an incident in the school or community, when issues of racism will need to be tackled directly. Drama and role-play are powerful ways of giving children some insight and understanding of these matters. Theatre in Education groups and Development Education Centres can provide materials and starting points. A number of useful INSET books make suggestions about how teachers can deal with these matters sensitively (see for example Epstein and Sealey, 1990 and Brown et al, 1990).

Assessment

One explanation for underachievement by ethnic minority pupils could lie in the assessment procedures themselves. These are largely decided by the educational establishment – examination boards, SCAA and senior staff. The assessment of bilingual learners through English medium tests and exams has an effect on their performance. Assessment procedures can discriminate against ethnic minority students, whether or not they are fully fluent in English.

Teachers make informal assessments of learners almost continuously. We decide whether a situation demands our intervention, whether to suggest that a pupil rewrites a piece of work, which group a child should work in and which of a number of resources s/he should be offered. We advise pupils about option choices and exam syllabuses. All these decisions are based on professional, but in part subjective, judgements of pupil's behaviour, attitude, performance and ability. They depend to a great extent on our own feelings, values and educational philosophies, which we rarely examine or make explicit.

Evaluation and assessment form a vital part of teaching. They inform the planning and review process and should be an important aspect of curriculum development. At their best teacher assessments are dynamic, informed and detailed ways of feeding back on pupils' progress. We should, however be aware of how our own attitudes can influence and affect the judgements we make. Wright (1987), for example, has shown how teachers' attitudes can affect the placing of black students in particular bands, streams and option groups. She shows how these judgements, often based on the pupils' behaviour rather than performance, has significant influence on their future attainment. We need to be more accountable for the decisions that we make.

More formal and so-called objective assessment is not without its problems. Bias can affect test procedures in a number of ways. Pupils' attitudes to the assessment process can affect outcomes. Learners who are diligent and persistent and who make the effort to 'learn the rules' of assessment are more likely to succeed. Some students and their families will place great importance on results and on movement through the levels; others will see it as irrelevant to their situation.

A great deal of research has been carried out into the different ways in which test design favours boys or girls. The APU (Assessment of Performance Unit) found that girls achieve on essay-type questions, whereas boys do better in a multiple choice format. Girls respond better to questions which are set in a social context and boys to more abstract examples. Boys excel in mechanical and manipulative skills. There is rather less evidence on ethnicity-based differences.

The ability to respond appropriately to a particular question or test item may partly depend on the pupil's previous experience. Gregory and Kelly (1994) give an example from research in the United States;

> Anglo-American children have very different discourse styles from the Afro-American minority group. The majority children use... a 'topic-centred' approach where talk focuses on one particular topic, whereas the minority children's talk is 'topic-associating' where a number of topics radiate from an initial theme. In a standardised test only one approach... could score as logical.' (p 205)

Children who are asked to make predictions of which items will sink or float before performing an experiment, will draw on their knowledge of the examples offered. Children may be used to different ways of organising and classifying what they know, so one child might see an engine and four carriages as one train and another see it as five separate vehicles.

So before we can interpret outcomes we must understand how they may give a false picture of true ability.

Standardised tests, too are likely to give inaccurate information. Many of the tests were originally standardised on white, middle class populations and are unsuitable for other pupils. This is particularly true of reading tests, which can give a distorted and over-simplified view of children's reading abilities.

The majority of standardised tests are normative, allowing comparison with results from different groups at different times by ranking them around the average. TGAT (1987), aware of the potential problems of normative tests, recommended a move toward criterion-referencing. They advocated clear criteria by which pupils' attainment was to be judged. The information from such tests is more useful to teachers and pupils, although comparability becomes more problematic. Questions still need to be asked about the appropriateness of such criteria and who decides what they are and, in effect, criterion-referencing can give rise to a disguised set of norms. Criteria need to be chosen which are flexible and reflect changing school populations.

A further form of assessment is ipsative, or self-assessment. This is a way in which pupils can reflect on their own learning and contribute to the assessment of their progress. Records of Achievement are partly based on this approach to assessment, giving pupils a chance to decide what to include in their portfolio. They can involve parents and others in the discussion of pupil attainment. The Primary Learning Record (Hester, 1993) provides a way of incorporating information from parents and others. However, schools and teachers risk intruding into areas of life that have hitherto been private and personal. There is also evidence that employers and further education institutions are less interested in RoAs as evidence of attainment than in examination results. Portfolios are therefore sometimes relegated to second rank in assessment priorities.

The most obvious way in which assessment methods can fail to indicate accurately the achievement of ethnic minority pupils is in the way in which they assess language alongside knowledge and skills. Pupils who are still struggling to express themselves fluently in English will take longer and will demonstrate their cognitive development less clearly than their more fluent peers. It may, therefore, be more difficult to assess their understanding. In addition most forms of assessment fail to give credit to just those aspects of learning at which bilinguals are skilled. Most assessment is product rather than process oriented – outcomes are more important than ways of reaching them. Yet bilingual learners often show impressive ability in the process of learning and problem-solving, although the end results may compare unfavourably with that of their peers. In particular, one of the outcomes measured is usually linguistic, either oral or literate. Because receptive understanding generally precedes productive ability a bilingual learner may be able to perform a task and understand the implications before s/he can express it all in words.

Most assessment is individual and personal, offering few opportunities for pupils to be credited for their contribution to a group effort. And yet this is precisely the kind of task at which bilinguals are very likely to succeed and make important and innovative contributions. Tests which rely on the production of English and do not allow children to demonstrate their awareness of language and their developing knowledge about languages as systems and means of communication disadvantage bilingual learners and fail to validate the positive aspects of bilingualism.

In terms of the day to day decisions that affect a child's learning teacher assessment will still be the most important. But these judgements must be supported by evidence. Observation and sampling are the best way to build up a record over time of a pupil's achievements. Relying on simple checklists of what children can, or more usually, cannot do is unhelpful. Even checklists can lead to negative thinking about a child's abilities. Simply to indicate on a piece of paper that on a particular date a child was unable to differentiate between right and left, for example, gives no indication of the context for the learning. Nor does it explain the support for understanding or suggest why the pupil did not show this ability. It does not tell the teacher anything helpful about what should be done.

We need to build in systems that ensure regularity of observation and monitoring of success. We must provide opportunities for pupils to show what they can do in different contexts and over time. Listening to learners and recording their strategies for problem-solving will provide valuable evidence about their attainments and about how to plan for their development. Drummond (1993) suggests that we are more successful when we look back and review recent achievements than when we plan long term programmes which may fail to respond to pupils' needs. This process of review needs to be analytical and based on descriptions of what pupils actually say and do and it must inform future planning.

Plans that are made following observations and monitoring may involve changes in classroom practices. Cummins' framework, which advocates moving from cognitively undemanding and context-embedded toward cognitively demanding and context-reduced tasks is a useful model. It depends, however, on teachers understanding what is cognitively demanding for each child and what a relevant context might be. There is a danger of making unfounded assumptions. All our pupils require a challenging learning situation and it may be more helpful to adopt a framework which guides us towards asking relevant questions about assessment which we can then build into our planning.

One questions is likely to be: 'how will I enable learners to assess their own progress?' Teachers have tried different approaches. They include conferences which can be set up between teachers and individual pupils or with groups of pupils, with or without a teacher. *Conferences* can enable learners to think about their progress and understanding and to articulate what they need to do in order to move forward. Graves (1983) developed the use of conferences with young writers, who became skilled at sharing problems and solutions with each other and providing sensitive insights into the writing process. Conferences create time when a teacher can give undivided attention to one pupil.

Journals can provide a written dialogue between teacher and pupil and thus require a minimal level of literacy. They have the advantage of providing models in a relatively permanent but unthreatening form. Journals or logs are also a record for the pupil of what s/he has learnt during a session or lesson and a form of practice and reflection which can be helpful.

Self-assessment can be built into planning for a whole class. Pupils can complete a questionnaire or tick chart at the beginning of a topic and a similar one at the end and so compare how their attitudes have changed or what new knowledge they have acquired. Before starting a topic about Indian history, for example, one class of secondary pupils noted what they knew about India. At the end of the topic a longer response was asked for. This provided evidence of learning and changed attitudes for both the pupils and the teachers.

TGAT (1987) specifically allows for assessment in the pupil's first language 'wherever practicable' (para 53). The practicability obviously depends on the number of languages spoken and whether there is a bilingual teacher or other assistance. However, even were the practical difficulties overcome, testing in first language is not always desirable. As Shan (1990) explains: 'Assessment in mother tongue alone can only be appropriate for what is learnt in mother tongue' (p.17).

If children are learning about chemical reactions, say, or the history of the Victorians or the ways in which different shapes fit together, it may well be that they only have the relevant specialist vocabulary in the language in which they were taught. Bilingual teachers are often concerned mainly with ensuring that pupils understand the concepts and grasp the English terminology and other bilingual adults may find the translation of specialist terminology, as well as the assessment itself, beyond their training.

It is possible for teachers to assess pupils whose language they do not share but they must provide opportunities for learners to demonstrate their understanding through how they approach and engage with practical activities, respond to carefully structured questions and interact in the classroom. They also have to listen to what pupils and others tell us about their learning.

We do our pupils an injustice if we do not prepare them for SATs and the other external assessment tasks that they will be required to undertake. We need to introduce the language of exams so that pupils can anticipate some of what they will be asked to do. We may need to practice examination situations and techniques so that the shock of the unknown is ameliorated. Many teachers and departments have produced simple flow charts and diagrams to give pupils some insight into how to tackle a written examination.

Teachers must recognise that: 'Assessment is essentially provisional, partial, tentative, exploratory and, inevitably, incomplete' (Drummond, (1993, p.14) and must establish suitable, systematic practices to take account of this. Teachers need to be clear about the tasks they plan and the expectations they hold. We must develop ways of assessing thinking and learning and encourage pupils to engage with us in reflecting on their achievements. We must ensure that activities are well designed and supported by practical examples and tasks and, while being well-scaffolded, are sufficiently challenging to be just a little beyond what children are capable of on their own. In recording these activities we must focus on success rather than failure. And in making judgements that will affect our pupils we must ensure that a variety of evidence is available and open to scrutiny and moderation.

Teachers still retain a large degree of autonomy in the classroom and therefore carry a great responsibility for pupils' learning. Securing high achievement for all is part of this responsibility and explanations which ignore the contribution of classroom organisation and the management and assessment of learning can reinforce a deficit view of bilingual learners.

Chapter 6

Policies and Practice

Policies can be generated at various levels and take a variety of forms. The government, while claiming to be in favour of decentralisation, has issued directives which have major policy implications and which constrain and even determine what those policies should be. The National Curriculum in particular has required schools to formulate policies on the distribution of resources – money, staff and time – for different areas of the curriculum, on the role and nature of assessment and how it is to be prioritised, recorded and managed and on staff development. The Education Reform Acts of 1986 and 1988 gave new powers to governing bodies which have major policy implications for those bodies themselves and for the schools for which they have responsibility. The establishment of grant-maintained status and the way in which GMS schools are financed has led to fundamental reconsideration of local authority policies, for example, regarding school closure and amalgamation.

Local management of schools (LMS) has greatly diminished local education authority influence and control. In the past LEAs had policies on equality, for example, which their schools were obliged to implement but today such policies are only advisory. Clearly, the extent and way in which schools did in fact respond to LEA policy directives varied, but there were teams of inspectors or advisors who could support and direct practice in schools. Now these teams are reduced both in size and in influence and are bought in by schools to provide such services as they require.

Powers granted to schools under LMS, such as formula funding, have similarly affected policies. Schools now have a large measure of control over their own budgets, which are determined according to a formula closely related to pupil numbers. This creates an incentive for schools to adopt policies which will be attractive to parents and prospective parents, sometimes to the detriment of certain sections of the population such as ethnic minorities, who may be 'expensive', or lower ability pupils who may not enhance the school's performance in published results and league tables. Linked to this, delegated powers for staffing can lead to the adoption of particular policies about appointment and dismissal which have implications for class size, curriculum balance and provision of other resources which have a call on the budget.

An imminent Ofsted inspection can give rise to frantic policy-writing, but the inspection guidelines specify few policy requirements. Inspectors expect schools to provide a pre-inspection commentary so that they can place current practice and achievement in context, but there are few indications of what policies might be expected. The Handbook mentions marking, examination entrance, health and sex education and staffing, for example, but leaves to individual schools decisions about what policies they consider necessary. Inspectors are skilled at looking for evidence of the realities that lie behind the pieces of paper, so a policy that 'has been written by the few and ignored by the many' will soon be seen for what it is and disregarded for lack of effect on practice.

Recent changes to the Framework for Inspection removed the separate Equal Opportunities sections and replaced them with guidance that inspectors should be aware of issues affecting: ïthe full range of age, gender, attainment, special educational need, ethnicity and background' (OFSTED, 1995 para 11). It is unfortunate that the general experience schools have of inspections does not inspire confidence in the ability of teams to respond to this guidance.

Forming policies

Despite cause for a certain cynicism about the value of policies there are a number of advantages in having these bits, or sometimes reams, of paper. Firstly, the process of arriving at the policy can be enlightening and educational, even if at times, painful. The discussions, the airing and sharing views, the challenging and changing of opinions, can rekindle enthusiasm and be a genuine learning experience. It can involve staff and others in the school in a joint activity that has potential for consolidation and empowerment. The participation can in itself have significant ramifications.

When people come together to plan something, there is obvious value to them in the feedback, skill development, social interaction and knowledge growth that they receive. More than this, participation usually fosters a commitment in people to the results or product (Corson, 1993, p.154).

Without this commitment or ownership, even the best policies are destined for failure through lack of implementation. But it follows that only the people who are involved in the discussion and formulation of the policy are likely to feel committed so anyone who has not been involved, whether from choice or circumstance, needs to be considered, consulted and informed. This has important implications for management in terms of delegation and responsibility and for review and evaluation.

A second benefit of policies is that they serve as a point of reference, a base line, a statement of 'where we stand' on particular issues. They provide written evidence of a set of values that the school, department or group espouses. They are a fall-back position in situations of conflict or indecision. Their existence or absence indicates certain priorities and underlying assumptions. The language in which documents are couched can be very revealing of attitudes towards pupils and parents, towards learning and towards staff involvement.

Policies must be public. Policies of which only certain groups of people are aware are ineffective and divisive. If they are to be shared they must be clear and concise. They should not be open to abuse or misinterpretation. They should avoid the sort of jargon that excludes non-professionals. General 'mission statements' can be as bland as they are worthy. It needs to be clear from the policy what the practical implications might be. A statement which everyone can agree with, interpret as they please and put to one side, is not worth the paper it is written on.

Thirdly, policies provide an opportunity for action. The strength of any policy lies in its implementation and its capacity to enable people to respond effectively in particular situations. It provides a way of acting in a planned and consistent, rather than an ad hoc, manner. Such consistency is part of what is implied in equality, for if different people can make subjective and uninformed judgements about appropriate behaviours instead of following agreed criteria, then unfair treatment becomes a real possibility.

A negative model

In 1986 Ahmed Iqbal Ullah was murdered by a white pupil in the playground of Burnage High School in Manchester. The resulting inquiry into the events surrounding the murder was finally published in 1989 (Macdonald, 1989). Both Burnage High School and Manchester Education Authority had anti-racist policies but they did not prevent Ahmed's murder nor alleviate the racist environment in which it occurred. This failure can be attributed, at least in part, to inadequacies in all three aspects that have been identified as crucial to effective policy making. The process by which the policy was arrived at involved only a small group of people who were regarded with suspicion or even hostility by some of those who would have to implement the proposals. The policy-makers had the nominal power but not always the influence to ensure implementation. Nor did they command the loyalty that would have made implementation effective. A working party had earlier drafted a document which was circulated to staff for comment and subsequently amended and adopted. This policy was found, after a few years, to be ineffective in that it failed to address significant areas matters as pastoral issues and community liaison. The body set up to draft a new policy, called the Ethnic Minority Advisory Group, was made up of black parents. Because black pupils were the victims of racism, management had decided that the best way to give them a voice was through such an advisory group. The lack of involvement of white parents and pupils created divisions and distrust that proved disastrous. According to the Burnage Report: 'It is clear that any anti-racist policy... will be totally ineffective if carried out in a vacuum, *without the involvement of parents and students.*' (Macdonald, 1989, p.351, original emphasis)

The policy that was in place when Ahmed was murdered gave no guidance as to action or interpretation and could be ignored by those who wished to do so without fear of repercussions. Some of the staff and students most affected were not even aware of its existence. Evidence was presented to the committee about the inconsistencies in their response to racism by members of staff. Some made it clear that they would not tolerate racist language or behaviour, others condoned racism by ignoring it and a minority of staff appear to have contributed to it by their own actions. Senior management seem to have been committed to tackling racism and introduced various measures such as supporting multicultural education and employing Section 11 teachers. Nevertheless the policies provided neither guidance nor pressure for action and, despite their existence, the school remained extremely racist.

Burnage serves as a tragic example of how policies in themselves can be an irrelevance. If pieces of paper cannot tell us anything useful about practice it might be more useful to start with practice and see what that can tell us about policies. HMI and Ofsted recommend that schools begin with an audit of what is in place in order to identify the gaps and decide priorities. Certainly we can tell a great deal about the underlying philosophy and attitudes in a school by seeing how staff, parents and pupils interact, whether the environment is lively and geared towards learning and what resources are being used.

Starting from practice

This way of looking at policy is similar to Elmore's process of 'backward mapping' (Elmore, 1989). In most situations, he suggests, policies are formed by starting with a statement of intent. Consideration is then given to how to implement the statement and what sort of outcomes to expect. The assumption behind such a 'forward mapping' model is that policy makers have control over the implementation. But this can rarely, if ever, be the case. Some of those who have to implement policies may not have had the opportunity to be involved in their formulation, others may have had no interest, time or desire to do so. Rather than 'forward mapping', Elmore suggests that we need to start by agreeing on the behaviours that need to be modified. Firstly, we need to identify cause for concern. Only then can the organisational operations leading to change can be identified and a policy statement be formulated. Thus policies are generated from practice and not the other way round.

The need for change can come about in various ways. It can be a response to external requirements such as National Curriculum orders, which are statutory and imposed. Other changes are externally available, such as the decision to adopt a particular reading scheme. This will reflect and affect reading policy. Yet other changes are internally generated. Whatever the imperative it is fruitless to attempt to change the unalterable. Sometimes those who plan change are too far from the implementation to understand what is and is not possible. Moreover, implementation requires not only sound principles and logical arguments but also resources in terms of training, time, equipment and personnel. As Fullan (1989) states:

> ...the major things that must be done:opportunity for training and interaction during implementation, good programme development or selection, allowance for redefinition of the change, a two or three year time

perspective, supportive principals and the like. The response to that list is frequently along the lines that it is impossible to do this or that because of lack of time, lack of resources and so on. I then say, 'Well don't expect much implementation to occur.' (p 206)

We must accept that change takes time, involves uncertainty and can cause anxiety. It may also necessitate the learning of new skills and therefore training and trialling must be incorporated. It requires the right balance of pressure and support in order to be successful. The process is rarely smooth and can meet opposition at various stages. There may be direct or indirect criticism, obstruction and prevarication. Strategies will have to be evolved to deal with opposition and to convince those who need to be convinced. Support will need to be sought from various quarters. Enormous effort may need to be put into dissemination and review and amendment. But the most important feature of any policy will be its outcomes. What does it do?

The most effective policies are often those generated from the 'bottom-up' through an understanding of the need for change and a desire for action rather than rhetoric. Policies generated in this way may not seem dramatic and are frequently small scale but the effects are cumulative. Perhaps more effective than the 'cascade' is the 'ripple' approach – instead of being dribbled down from the few at the top to those at the chalk face, these start in a small way and gradually draw in more and more of the people concerned.

Gathering allies

Hughes (1993) describes how she began introducing equal opportunities in a small way in her classroom. She was aware of the potential for resistance from certain staff and parents, so her first steps were to augment the class resources with appropriate books and posters and to invite visitors from the local community to run music sessions and dance workshops. At the same time she made sure that the results did not go unnoticed. She talked about them to colleagues and displayed them around the school. Later she was able to involve sympathetic colleagues in similar work. She formed alliances with black governors and encouraged them to attend an LEA training session on equal opportunities. Areas of concern in the school centred around discipline and class management and Hughes linked these to equal opportunities and the achievement of black pupils. This brought the issues to a whole-school forum, where equal opportunities policy could be discussed and developed.

Questions about classroom support and the deployment of Section 11 staff can be raised in a similar way. Initially problems may be dealt with as they occur, but there are underlying policy issues which need to be addressed. Senior members of staff and opinion leaders in the school, not necessarily the same people, are crucial to this process. Take the example of a deputy head in a secondary school in the early 1980s who was resistant to working with a support teacher for reasons she never made explicit. Every time it was suggested that a Section 11 teacher be timetabled to work in her classroom, she found reasons why it would not be practicable. Finally she relented and found the experience proved less threatening and more helpful than she seemed to have anticipated. Being able to share the preparation and being relieved of some of the responsibility for bilingual learners began the conversion of a potentially hostile, or at least suspicious, but influential member of staff into an ally. It helped to pave the way towards a policy of mainstream support at a time when withdrawal was still the norm.

Clearly, then, involving relevant people in policy making does much to ensure success. We need to know who the relevant players are and be familiar with the many subtle and informal ways in which people can facilitate or hinder change, through manipulating meetings, lobbying and forming alliances (see Hoyle, 1989).

Broadening participation

Many documents about policy formulation imply or state that the participants are teachers and this is often the case. A need is identified and a working party is formed to consider the issues and draft a policy. This is presented to other staff, usually teachers but sometimes also support and non-teaching staff, for comment and amendment. Governors are invited to comment. A final version is then published for staff, governors, pupils and parents.

More recently the debate about who should be involved has broadened to include the local community. One of the failures of Burnage was due to the exclusion from policy-making of so many in the community and the school, specifically white pupils and their parents, from an issue in which they were both powerful and centrally concerned. Corson (1994) discusses the position of communities in developing bilingual language policies. The communities are, he argues, the experts and become empowered by their role in policy formation.

Observers of educational reform.... claim that policies of compensatory, multicultural and anti-racist education imposed from afar, make little difference to educational inequality.... Only a local community can really decide what is necessary' (Corson, 1994 p.15).

Mehmet Ali (1986) questions the reasons for advocating parental and community involvement. She argues that the motives of some people may be suspect and suggests a range of 'real' reasons which may underlie the rhetoric such as 'it looks good on your record', 'you want another perspective' or 'your local education authority or the government says you should'. It is rarely the case that schools as institutions are prepared for genuine sharing of power and they often 'back-off' when recommendations are not to their liking. As Siraj-Blatchford (1994) observes: 'Until parents can trust the educators there is little point in expecting their active support' (p.12).

More black and ethnic minority representatives are certainly needed on governing bodies. Yet procedures, formal and informal, effectively prevent this from happening. We need policy makers who will monitor and if necessary make changes to the structures themselves and this may mean giving more power to those directly affected by policies – to pupils and their parents.

One way in which a wider population can be involved in policies is in their review and evaluation. No policy lasts for ever and its practical effects will need to be monitored regularly. At this stage it is particularly important to elicit the views of those who are affected and to re-draft documents in the light of experience. Monitoring can reveal practices which have unexpected effects. For example, at one secondary school a system of removing pupils who were being disruptive was part of the behaviour policy. The process was well documented and publicised and pupils knew what the warnings and record cards implied. Staff were on duty to supervise pupils who were unable to remain in class. When this policy was reviewed most teachers felt that it was working well. It was only when the gender and ethnicity of those who were removed from class was monitored that evidence of wider concerns emerged with significant consequences for behaviour and equal opportunities policy and practice.

Schools will have many policies and all will affect pupils, including bilingual learners. But some are of particular significance for bilingual children and may determine how staff and other resources are deployed and how these pupils are perceived and included in the institution. Cummins

(1994) makes points about the Canadian system which are highly relevant to British education and which need to be seriously considered when forming policies. He identifies a number of serious constraints on the achievement of bilingual pupils:

- Policies at federal, state/provincial or local levels that fail to take account of the knowledge base that exists regarding students; for example, policies in the areas of special education, psychological assessment, streaming/tracking, entry and exit criteria for bilingual or ESL programs all systematically discriminate against ESL students.
- Teacher education institutions that continue to treat issues related to ESL students as marginal and that send new teachers into the classroom with minimal information regarding patterns of language and emotional development among students and few pedagogical strategies for helping students learn.
- Curriculum that reflects only the experiences and values of the middle-class white native-English-speaking population and effectively suppresses the experiences and values of ESL students.
- The absence from most schools of professionals capable of communicating in the languages of students and their parents: such professionals could assist in functions such as home language instruction, literacy tutoring, home language assessment for purposes of placement and intervention, and parent/school liaison.
- Criteria for promotion to positions of responsibility that take no account of the individual's experience with or potential for leadership in the education of ESL students.' (p 34)

Language policies

The National Curriculum presents a form of linguicism in which English is equated with language. As Brumfit (1995) argues, all language development is expected to take place through English and the only bilingualism that is recognised is Welsh. All other language provision is treated as 'foreign' language learning, which carries with it certain assumptions about range, content, purpose and pedagogy. So the attitudes a school takes towards bilingual learners will need to be very carefully considered and clarified in its language policy.

We have seen that research and experience over several years and many countries gives powerful support for the continued use and development of first languages in education. Continuing proficiency in both languages will have intellectual advantages for bilingual learners and will affect their social and personal identity. Moreover, the development of English language skills is improved rather than impaired by the use of first language for learning. Schools therefore need to determine how to make first language maintenance a reality, not merely transitional but central to the education of bilingual pupils.

Discussions about which of several languages to begin with and how they can be most effectively supported must involve the local communities affected, but no discussion can ignore the feelings and suggestions of people who feel that they and their children might be disadvantaged by such a policy. There will be resourcing and timetabling implications. Most schools will find it difficult to make the necessary provision and may feel it is only possible to make a small scale beginning. Inner city schools are increasingly introducing first language support and tuition and their advice and support might be helpful. Expertise resides in the local community.

Even if community languages cannot be taught at this stage, the language policy needs to indicate the desirability of moving towards this position and to indicate proposals for the interim. Including such aims in the school development plan will affect appointments, INSET and budget decisions. The policy will include ways of incorporating first languages into all four language areas – speaking, listening, reading and writing – and will be a way of encouraging Year group and curriculum leaders to re-examine their practice and to raise the issues in their meetings. The way in which PACT schemes are introduced, for example or the literature studied at GCSE will reflect the thought given to first language use.

Corson (1990) suggests three main headings under which to consider language policy: organisation and management; staff approaches to language and curriculum concerns. A language policy will have to take account of staff allocation, appointment and training. The role of the language co-ordinator may need to be considered and the job description discussed. In secondary schools Heads of Modern Languages, English, Learning Support and the pastoral curriculum will all be involved and their responsibilities may need to be clarified or redefined. Support teachers, whether bilingual, special educational needs or ESL, have an important role, as do assistants, primary helpers and outside agencies. On the wider level, community and parental participation will be an issue, both formally, as on the PTA and governing body, and informally. Matters of translation and interpretation will be considered.

Thought is also needed about the nature of pupil involvement in matters of language policy and how to elicit their views. Organisational aspects such as the placement of bilingual learners in particular classes or option groups and the deployment of support for them will need to be considered. The collection, collation, storage and access to records and the monitoring of pupil achievement will be incorporated into the policy.

Staff awareness of language issues will determine some of the starting points for the policy and may have training implications. The acceptance of the value of language diversity and an agreement to promote it will need to underpin a language policy, although inevitably enthusiasm will vary.

Curriculum issues will be concerned not only with content but with pedagogy. Factors which need to be considered include:

- the importance of talk and the encouragement of first language
- ways to teach and develop reading and writing skills
- how to respond to children's writing
- encouraging writing for real purposes and a variety of audiences
- publication and display of pupils' work
- assessment of language skills, including first language
- access to public examinations and accreditation

Equal opportunities policies

There are differences of opinion about whether to adopt a holistic approach to equal opportunities or to tackle the issue on separate fronts and write policies specific to race, gender, disability etc. Doing the latter is likely to lead to repetition and possibly omission, but it may achieve the involvement of more people. Patrick and Burke (1993) argue that:

> by far the most effective way ....is to ensure that equal opportunities is treated in a holistic fashion, by the creation of a generalised statement of intent which makes particular reference to the full range of equal opportunities issues (p. 202).

Gaine (1989) is less convinced, suggesting that in practice different issues appear to have priority at different times and that policies are generated in direct response. A piecemeal approach may in fact produce more effective results and lessons learnt from one document may be helpful in drafting and implementing another. Whichever route is followed there are clearly links between policies which address issues of race inequality and those which deal with gender, sexuality, class or disability.

The notion of equality itself requires clarification. To some it implies treating all children the same and there are teachers who claim not to notice the difference between their pupils but to adopt a 'colour-blind' approach. This position is very hard to sustain. Evidence shows that teachers who claim to treat all children alike, rarely do so in reality. Even if they did this would hardly be just. Failure to provide ramps for wheel-chairs or left-handed scissors for children who need them, is as discriminatory as offering all children the same lunch-time diet or demanding adherence to identical uniform rules. Justice demands that relevant differences are treated differently. The question remains as to which are the relevant differences and the answer changes over time, indicating the importance of frequent policy reviews.

How we identify the evidence for equality of opportunity is hard to decide. One view is that we should seek equality of outcome and look at exam results, for example, noting the performance of different groups of pupils. Genuine equality of opportunity, in this view, would result in outcomes which showed the same profile for all. It is not denied that there are individual differences and that certain people excel at some subjects. On average, however, achievements should be the same across ethnic groups.

A difficulty with this argument lies in the steps that might be needed to achieve parity and whether outcomes give a true indication of equality. Children come to school and continue their education with very different experiences, abilities and interests. Bilingual learners in general have greater metalinguistic awareness than monolinguals, for instance. Are their abilities to be suppressed so they achieve the same results as their monlingual peers? Equal opportunities policies need to address issues of justice, fairness, recognition of differences and opposition to discrimination.

Policies tend to focus on particular issues:

- the general *ethos* of the school reflects positive views of, and attitudes to, cultural and racial differences.

- issues of *stereotyping, bias and omission* are confronted within the curriculum and resources
- a *curriculum* which values the range and variety of knowledge that pupils bring with them and aims to share, extend and build on this knowledge.
- *access* to the curriculum for bilingual learners provides support where needed in order to promote learning and achievement.
- teachers have information about the *languages* spoken by the children and used in the home.
- *parents and the wider community* are involved in the life of the school and the promotion of learning.
- *special provision* is made for religious observance, dress and diet where required.
- behaviour management includes particular attention to *racial harassment*

Racism takes many forms and may be covert or overt. It can be perpetrated by an individual or group or be a result of systems within the institution. If, for example, most black pupils are placed in a particular class, or seated in one area of the room, the effects if not the intention appear discriminatory and so can be racist. When pupils were withdrawn for language support, the fact that groups of children of ethnic minority backgrounds went to a different room, participated in a different curriculum and were taught by different staff, might well have been racist. It is racist for teachers consistently to mispronounce or misspell a pupil's name or for mid-day supervisors to insist that children eat proscribed food, even if they do so from ignorance or with benign intent.

Racism within institutions can extend to black staff as well as students. Teachers whose qualifications are not recognised, although they may have years of experience and training abroad, often have low status and pay and their training opportunities may be limited. Where ancillary staff are recruited from the local community by word of mouth, positions can often be passed from mother to daughter or, more rarely, father to son, without being advertised and so are closed to more recent arrivals. Senior staff who are black describe the opposition they have to overcome because of their race not their ability, and how they frequently have very little support. One recently appointed black head in a predominantly white area describes how she felt inhibited from devoting resources to her own training and support when the rest of the staff pressed for other urgent priorities within the school and how this heightened her sense of isolation within the LEA.

Overt racism, too takes many forms. Black pupils describe the daily harassment; the sly kicks, nudges and remarks under the breath, that they endure. Possessions are removed or tampered with 'just for fun'. Many learn that it is fruitless to mention such incidents to staff or to 'make a fuss'. Bullying and harassment in the playground are ignored or simply missed by staff and complaints often bring reprisals. The use of derogatory terms and jokes, name-calling and mimicking accents are not uncommon. Name-calling is not to be taken lightly, especially abuse of someone's parentage, race or religion. All verbal and physical abuse must be challenged and every school needs clear guidelines about how to deal with both the perpetrator and the victim. It is essential that victims know what action is being taken on their behalf and do not feel punished for their vulnerability.

Special educational needs policies

With the reduction in funding for Section 11 staff and the tendency for more of them to be managed by schools rather than by central teams, it is not always clear where to place support teachers within the school management structure. Often they are included within learning support or special needs departments. Although most teachers recognise that bilingualism is not a learning difficulty (see Cinamon and Gravelle, 1988) some argue that the nature of the support required is similar to that given to pupils who have special educational needs.

Policies will need to distinguish very clearly between learning 'difficulties' and language 'difficulties' and set up procedures to assess them. Cloud (1994) suggests how we can make assessments which do not automatically locate lack of achievement with the learner. We need:

* an understanding of the pupil's present knowledge and skills, in her/his first language, and also in other areas relevant to education and schooling
* to assess the pupil's ability and determine whether s/he has a physical or mental impairment or medical condition that affects learning
* to take account of, emotional or other factors may affect motivation
* to be aware of the opportunities the pupil has had to develop conceptual and linguistic skills.

The problem remains as to how to make assessments that are fair to bilingual learners and a true reflection of their ability, potential and needs. Standard tests and assessment instruments for the identification of learning difficulties are inappropriate for bilingual learners mainly because lack of fluency in English can disguise their ability and understanding. Additionally, as we have seen, tests have cultural biases which disadvantage pupils from certain backgrounds.

It can sometimes be helpful to make assessments in first languages. Certain disabilities such as sensory or physical difficulties, are likely to show across languages. However, caution is still needed. Some abilities that are more easily expressed in L2 than in L1, for example reading skills may be less well developed in one language so practices will need to vary accordingly. Administration and interpretation of first language assessment is a skilled process and suitable bilingual professionals will not always be available.

A small number of tests have been standardised on bilingual populations, but their use remains specific to that population. Some educational psychologists have devised tests which are useful for the assessment of bilingual learners (see Cline and Frederickson, 1991) but misidentification continues to be a serious concern. Curriculum based assessment gives a fuller and fairer picture of learners' abilities. Hall (1995) suggests a programme of screening, information collection, observation and sampling, before decisions are made about Special Educational Needs. This takes time and no decision should be made within the first few months of admission. In any case a bilingual learner will continue to need support for language development, whatever other provision is deemed necessary.

The DFE issued a Code of Practice on the Identification and Assessment of Special Educational Needs (DFE, 1994) which sets out clear procedures for consultation and provision. The role of the Special Needs Co-ordinator is crucial in ensuring that the requirements are fulfiled and it may well fall to her/him to determine whether bilingual learners are included in this provision. There will be some bilingual pupils who have learning difficulties, but one would not expect a greater proportion than in the monolingual population and careful monitoring will be needed to check that this is the case.

Special Educational Needs policies therefore need to consider how to identify, assess and support bilingual learners who are found to have learning difficulties. The process of consultation requires particular attention since parents will have to be given very clear information in order to be as fully involved as the Code of Practice requires. Translation and interpretation are helpful, but even when first languages are used, parents will not always be familiar with the terms and aims behind special provision nor understand what the various categories of provision and legal status imply.

Policies need to make clear distinctions between the majority of bilingual learners who do not have learning difficulties and the few who do. The distinction should be reiterated and reinforced whenever necessary to correct any misunderstandings on the part of staff, parents or pupils. The status and organisation of support for bilingual learners gives a clear indication of the attitude of school management and staff towards them.

Practical implications – start here and now

Making policy sounds rather grand and important. It appears to be beyond the capacity or responsibility of classroom teachers, except perhaps through membership of working parties or staff meetings. Yet the best and most effective policies emanate from thoughtful practice and we are all practitioners. Change can occur if we start immediately, even if at first it is only on a small scale. We need to be pragmatic about what it is we can do and think carefully about our priorities. We will need allies, so discussion and dissemination will be important to increase participation. Displaying the outcomes of some curriculum innovation, for example, can raise children's esteem and provide a model for other teachers. Exhibitions or booklets which are accompanied by a summary of the process by which they came about can be helpful. More informal discussions, particularly where there is evidence of children's achievement, will have sometimes imperceptible but nonetheless real effects.

Innovations which are planned, evaluated and disseminated can influence others and form the basis of policies. All that is required is that we become systematic and 'reflective practitioners' or action researchers. One of the best ways to do this is through partnership teaching.

Partnership teaching

Partnership teaching is a development from earlier models of support and team teaching (see Bourne and McPake, 1991). It was developed specifically to provide more effective support for bilingual learners, but its implications extend to learning for all pupils. It has been interpreted and operated in different ways in different institutions. At its best it becomes part of a whole school approach to teaching and learning. Teachers work together usually through teaching whole classes, but also in preparing teaching materials, planning and organising lessons and evaluating pupils' achievements and their own collaboration. Its aim is to develop and deliver a curriculum that meets the needs of all pupils through sharing the expertise and experience which teachers bring to the classroom.

> In a school which is developing its links with the community, Partnership Teaching will involve not only teachers and teaching assistants, but will draw on wider Partnerships by involving parents, other adults and community groups; and it will bring in primary-secondary and home-school liaison partnerships. (Bourne and McPake, 1991)

Partners begin by identifying the area within the classroom that they wish to develop together. This may be for part of the week, for a whole term or course or only for one lesson or session. It may involve an aspect of the curriculum or focus on particular materials or teaching strategies. The planning is then collaborative: the partners set objectives, decide on organisation, plan materials and each take responsibility for particular aspects of the teaching. An important part of this planning concerns pupils' learning and partners will have to agree on how to assess and record achievement. The achievements of pupils and of the partnership itself will be evaluated and changes made as necessary. The final part of the cycle is the dissemination phase, which can form part of INSET and staff development.

Partnership Teaching is a particular form of action research which is supportive because it involves colleagues. The opportunity for joint reflection and analysis is very helpful, but even if partnerships cannot be developed then other forms of action research are still possible. Action research is based on the principle that teachers continue to be learners. The best teachers learn continually from their pupils and colleagues. They notice what succeeds and think about the reasons for success and failure. They refuse to become mindless operators of a predetermined and predigested curriculum.

Action research is a way of making practice more systematic and focused. It is based on the constructivist model of learning, but applied to teachers – that we can all take responsibility for our knowledge about and interpretation of the world and that we can act on the basis of this knowledge. A learning teacher will not accept what others define as 'good practice', 'effective assessment' or a 'sound curriculum' but treat these judgements as problematic and find his/her own evidence in the learning of the pupils. By investigating what 'works', teachers may arrive at generalisations, supported by evidence, which can then inform practice and ultimately policy.

We need the confidence to start now, even if we start in a small way. We will need to talk about what is happening in our classrooms, schools and communities, to identify allies and begin to convert opponents. Together we must prioritise concerns and possibilities for change and not waste energy pursuing the unattainable or berating ourselves for not doing more. We need to retain a belief that change is desirable and that despite all the pressures upon us and that it is possible. Acquiring relevant information and developing our own learning will be crucial. We must remain open-minded and be prepared to listen, particularly to those whose experiences must inform policies for bilingual learners. And we must be rigorous in monitoring the effects of policies and practices and willing to admit our mistakes and make changes accordingly. By improving our own practice we will better support all our pupils and particularly the bilingual learners in our schools.

Teachers have always planned for learning and monitored their own practice and the contribution that this makes to pupil achievement. The presence of bilingual learners in our schools and classrooms makes it even more urgent that we continue to be active and reflective. This book has sought to assist teachers in that reflection and to make suggestions about action. It has described how children learn language and the conditions that enhance their learning of further languages. It has suggested how schools can value and support pupils' first languages. The education of bilingual pupils is about more than their acquisition of English and the contribution that first language development can make to that process. It is about ensuring that all pupils have access to good education that will extend their abilities and challenge their thinking.

Bibliography

Ada, A F (1988) The Pajaro Valley Experience in Skutnabb-Kangas, Tand Cummins, *J Minority Education*, Clevedon, Multilingual Matters

Afro-Caribbean Language and Literacy Project (1990) *Language and Power,* ILEA, Harcourt Brace Jovanovich

Alexander, R (1994) 'Analysing Practice' in Bourne, J (ed) *Thinking Through Primary Practice*, London, Routledge

Allwright, R (1987) 'Concluding comments' in Ellis, R (ed) *Second Language Acquisition in Context*, London, Prentice Hall International

Baddeley, P and Eddershaw, C (1994) *Not So Simple Picture Books*, Stoke-on-Trent, Trentham

Bain, R, Fitzgerald, B and Taylor, M (eds) (1992) *Looking into Language*, London, Hodder and Stoughton

Baker, C (1993) *Foundations of Bilingual Education and Bilingualism*, Clevedon, Multilingual Matters

Barnes, D (1976) *From Communication to Curriculum*, Harmondsworth, Penguin

Barnes, D, Britton, J, and Rosen, H (1969) *Language, the learner and the school*, Harmondsworth, Penguin.

Barnes, D and Todd, F (1977) *Communication and Learning in Small Groups*, London, Routledge and Kegan Paul

Barrs, M and Thomas, A (1991) *The Reading Book*, London, CLPE.

Beardsmore, H B (1986) *Bilingualism: Basic Principles*, Clevedon, Multilingual Matters

Bennett, N and Dunne, E (1992) *Managing Classroom Groups*, Hemel Hempstead, Simon and Schuster

Bialystok, E (ed) (1991) *Language Processing in Bilingual Children*, Cambridge, Cambridge University Press

Bialystok, E (1991) 'Metalinguistic dimensions of bilingual language proficiency' in Bialystok, E (ed) *Language Processing in Bilingual Children*, Cambridge, Cambridge University Press

Blackledge, A (1992) Education for Equality: Countering racism in the primary curriculum, *Multicultural Teaching* Vol 11 No 1

Blackledge, A (ed) (1994) *Teaching Bilingual Children*, Stoke-on-Trent, Trentham Books

Bourne, J (1989) *Moving into the Mainstream*, Windsor, NFER-Nelson

Bourne, J (ed) (1994) *Thinking through Primary Practice*, London, Routledge

Bourne, J and McPake, J (1991) *Partnership Teaching*, London, NFER/DES

Brandt, G (1986) *The Realisation of Anti-racist Teaching*, Lewes, Falmer Press

Brown, C, Barnfield, J and Stone, M (1991) *Spanner in the Works,* Stoke-on-Trent, Trentham Books

Brumfit, C, Ellis, R and Levine, J (eds) (1985) *English as a Second Language in the United Kingdom,* Oxford, Pergamon Press

Brumfit, C (ed)(1995) *Language Education in the National Curriculum*, Oxford, Blackwell

Bruner, J (1986) *Actual Minds, Possible Worlds*, London, Harvard University Press

Burgess-Macey, C (1994) Play in its Cultural Context, *Multicultural Teaching* Vol 12 No 2

Bush, T (ed) (1989) *Managing Education; Theory and Practice*, Milton Keynes, Open University Press

Canale, M (1984) 'On Some Theoretical Frameworks for Language Proficiency' in Rivera (ed) *Language Proficiency and Academic Achievement*, Clevedon, Multilingual Matters

Carby, H (1982) 'Schooling in Babylon' in Centre for Contemporary Cultural Studies, *The Empire Strikes Back,* London, Hutchinson

Carter, R (1990) *Knowledge About Language,* London, Hodder and Stoughton

Carty, P 'Vietdamned', *Guardian* 26.7.95

Central Advisory Council for Education (1967) *Children and their Primary Schools* (Plowden Report) London HMSO

Centre for Contemporary Cultural Studies (1982) *The Empire Strikes Back*, London, Hutchinson

Cinamon, D and Gravelle, M (1988) Bilingualism is NOT a learning difficulty, *Gnosis* 12

Claire, H, Maybin, J and Swann, J (eds) (1993) *Equality Matters* Clevedon, Multilingual Matters

Cline, T and Frederickson, N (1991) *Bilingual Pupils and the National Curriculum*, London, University College

Cloud, N (1994) 'Special Education Needs of Second Language Students' in Genesee, F (ed) *Educating Second Language Children*, Cambridge, Cambridge University Press

Coard, B (1971) *How the West Indian Child is made Educationally Sub-normal in the British School System*, London, New Beacon Books

Cole, M (ed) (1989) *Education for Equality,* London, Routledge

Collier, V (1989) How Long? A Synthesis of Research on Academic Achievement in a Second Language, *TESOL Quarterly* Vol 23 No 3

Commission for Racial Equality (1982) *Ethnic Minority Community Languages,* London CRE

Commission for Racial Equality (1986) *Teaching English as a Second Language*, Report of a Formal Investigation in Calderdale LEA., London C.R.E.

Corson, D (1990) *Language Policy across the Curriculum*, Clevedon, Multilingual Matters

Corson, D (1993) *Language, Minority Education and Gender,* Clevedon, Multilingual Matters

Corson, D (1994) 'Bilingual Education Policy and Social Justice' in Blackledge, A (ed) *Teaching Bilingual Children*, Stoke-on-Trent, Trentham Books

Crystal, D (1987) *The Cambridge Encyclopedia of Language*, Cambridge, Cambridge University Press

CUES Collaborative Learning Group (eds) (1988) *Collaborative Learning*, London, Centre for Urban Educational Studies

Cummins, J (1984) *Bilingualism and Special Education; Issues in Assessment and Pedagogy*, Clevedon, Multilingual Matters

Cummins, J (1986a) Bilingual Education and Anti-racist Education, *Interracial Books for Children Bulletin* Vol 17

Cummins, J (1986b) Empowering Minority Students, A Framework for Intervention, *Harvard Educational Review* Vol 56 No 1

Cummins, J (1991) 'Interdependence of first- and second-language proficiency in bilingual children' in Bialystok, E (ed) *Language Processing in Bilingual Children* Cambridge, Cambridge University P ress

Cummins, J (1994) 'Knowledge, Power and Identity in Teaching English as a Second Language', in Genesee, F (ed) *Educating Second Language Children*, Cambridge, Cambridge University Press

Cummins, J and Swain, M (1986) *Bilingualism in Education*, Harlow, Longman.

Curtis, S (1992) Peer tutoring, 'entitlement', 'access', and 'equal opportunities', *Multicultural Teaching* Vol 10 No 2

Davies, A and Sturman, E (eds) (1989) *Bilingual Learners in Secondary Schools*, London, Centre for Urban Educational Studies.

DES (1975) *A Language for Life*, (Bullock Report), London, HMSO

DES (1985) *Education for All: the Report of the Committee of Inquiry into the Education of Children from Ethnic Minority Groups* (Swann Report), London, HMSO

DES (1988) *Report of the Committee of Inquiry into the Teaching of the English Language*, (Kingman Report) London HMSO

DFE (1994) *Our Children's Education*, London, HMSO

DFE (1995) T*he National Curriculum Orders,* London, HMSO

Dhondy, F (1978) *Come to Mecca and other stories*, London, Fontana

Docherty, M (1991) A curriculum for all? *Language Matters*, Vol 3

Dodson, C.J (1985) Second Language Acquisition and Bilingual Development; A Theoretical Framework, *Journal of Multilingual and Multicultural Development* Vol 6 No 5

Donaldson, M (1978) *Children's Minds*, Glasgow, Fontana

Dorn, A and Hibbert, P (1987) 'Catch 22?: A look at the new Section 11 guidelines' in Section 11; Who Needs Special Funding? *Issues in Race and Education.* No 50

Doughty, P, Pearce, J and Thornton, G (1971) *Language in Use*, London, Edward Arnold

Drummond, M.J (1994) *Assessing Children's Learning*, London, David Fulton

Drummond, M J, Rouse, D and Pugh, G (1992) *Making Assessment Work*, Nottingham Group and National Children's Bureau

Dulay, H, Burt, M and Krashen, S (1982) *Language Two*, Oxford, Oxford University Press

Early, M (1990) Enabling first and second language learners in the classroom, *Language Arts* Vol 67 No 6

Edelsky, C et al (1983) Semilingualism and Language Deficit, *Applied Linguistics* Vol 4 No.1

Edwards, D and Mercer, N (1987) *Common Knowledge*, London, Methuen

Edwards, J (1994) *Multilingualism*, Harmondsworth, Penguin Books

Edwards, V (1995) 'The NALDIC Interview' in *NALDIC News* No 6

Edwards, V Goodwin, J and Wellings, A (1991) *English 7-14 Every Child's Entitlement*, London, David Fulton

Edwards, V and Redfern, A (1992) *The World in a Classroom*, Clevedon, Multilingual Matters

Eggleston, J (1985) The Educational and Vocational Experiences of Young Black Britons, *Multicultural Teaching* Vol 4 No 1

Eggleston, J Dunn, D and Anjali, M (1986) *Education for Some*, Stoke-on-Trent, Trentham Books

Ellis, R (1985) *Understanding Second Language Acquisition*, Oxford, Oxford University Press

Ellis, R (ed) (1987) *Second Language Acquisition in Context*, London, Prentice-Hall International

Elmore, R (1989) 'Backward Mapping: Implementation Research and Policy Decisions' in Moon, Murphy and Raynor (eds) *Policies for the Curriculum*, London, Hodder and Stoughton

Epstein, D (1993) *Changing Classroom Cultures*, Stoke-on-Trent, Trentham Books

Epstein, D and Sealey, A (1990) *Where it Really Matters*, Birmingham Development Education Centre

Fairclough, N (1989) *Language and Power*, London, Longman

Feuerverger, G (1994) A multicultural literacy intervention for minority language students, *Language and Education*, Vol 8 No 3

Fitzpatrick, B (1987) *The Open Door*, Clevedon, Multilingual Matters

Fitzpatrick, F (1994) *The Linguistic Background to ESL,* Bradford and Ilkley College

Flude, M and Hammer, M (eds) (1990) *The Education Reform Act 1988*, Lewes, Falmer Press

Frederickson, N and Cline, T (1990) *Curriculum Related Assessment with Bilingual Children,* London, University College

Fullan, M (1989) 'Planning, Doing and Coping with Change' in Moon, Murphy and Raynor, *Policies for the Curriculum*, London, Hodder and Stoughton

Gaine, C (1989) 'On getting equal opportunities policies and keeping them' in Cole (ed) *Education for Equality*, London, Routledge

Gaine, C (1995) *Still No Problem Here*, Stoke-on-Trent, Trentham Books

Galton, M (1989) *Teaching in the Primary School,* London, David Fulton

Genesee, F (ed) (1994) *Educating Second Language Children*, Cambridge, Cambridge University Press.

Gibbons, P (1991) *Learning to Learn in a Second Language*, Australia, Primary English Teaching Association.

Gill, D and Levidow, L (eds) (1987) *Anti-racist Science Teaching*, London, Free Association Books

Gill, D Mayor, B and Blair, M (eds) (1992) *Racism and Education*, London, Sage Publications

Gillborn, D (1990) *Race, Ethnicity and Education*, London, Unwin Hyman

Gillborn, D (1995) *Racism and Antiracism in Real Schools*, Buckingham, Open University Press

Gillham, B (1986) *The Language of School Subjects*, London, Heinemann

Gipps, C (1994) *Beyond Testing*, Lewes, Falmer Press

Gipps, C and Murphy, P (1994) *A Fair Test?* Buckingham, Open University Press

Glasersfeld, E von (1989) 'Learning as a Constructive Activity' in Murphy, P and Moon, B *Developments in Learning and Assessment*, London, Hodder and Stoughton.

Goodman, Y (1985) 'Kidwatching; Observing Children in the Classroom' in Jaggar, A and Smith-Burke, M *Observing the Language Learner*, International Reading Association

Graddol, D Cheshire, J and Swann, J (1994) *Describing Language,* Buckingham, Open University Press

Graham, J (1996) Using Illustration as the Bridge between Fact and Fiction, *English in Education,* Vol 30 No 1

Gravelle, M (1984) India; a study in development, *Multicultural Teaching* Vol 3 No 1

Gravelle, M (1989) Encouraging Questions, *Issues in Race and Education* No 56

Gravelle, M (1990) Assessment and bilingual pupils, *Multicultural Teaching* Vol 9 No 1

Gravelle, M (1992) To prove or improve? Assessment issues with particular reference to bilingual learners, *The Curriculum Journal* Vol 3 No 2

Gravelle, M and Sturman, E (1994) 'Assessing bilingual learners; issues of fluency' in Keel, P (ed) *Assessment in the Multi-ethnic Primary Classroom*, Stoke-on Trent, Trentham Books

Graves, D (1983) *Writing; Teachers and Children at Work,* Exeter, Heinemann

Gregory, E and Kelly, C (1994) 'Bilingualism and Assessment' in Bourne, J(ed) *Thinking Through Primary Practice*, London, Routledge.

Grosjean, F (1985) The Bilingual as a Competent but Specific Speaker-Hearer, *Journal of Multilingual and Multicultural Development* Vol 6 No.6

Hall, D (1995) *Assessing the Needs of Bilingual Pupils*, London, David Fulton

Halliday, M (1978) *Language as Social Semiotic*, London, Edward Arnold.

Harley, B et al (eds) (1990) *The Development of Second Language Proficiency*, Cambridge, Cambridge University Press.

Hart, S (1986) Evaluating Support Teaching, *Gnosis,* Vol 9

Hart, S (1992) Differentiation. Part of the problem or part of the solution? *The Curriculum Journal* Vol 3 No 2

Hawkins, E (1984) *Awareness of Language; an introduction*, Cambridge, Cambridge University Press

Heath, S (1983) *Ways with Words*, Cambridge,Cambridge University Press

Hester, H (1993) *Guide to the Primary Learning Record*, London, CLPE

Houlton, D and Willey, R (1983) *Supporting Children's Bilingualism*, York, Longman

Houlton, D (1985) *All Our Languages*, London, Edward Arnold

Hoyle, E (1989) 'The micropolitics of schools' in Bush (ed) *Managing Education; Theory and Practice,* Milton Keynes, Open University Press

Hughes, J (1993) 'Starting Points' in Claire, Maybin and Swann *Equality Matters*, Clevedon, Multilingual Matters

Ifrah, G (1985) *From One to Zero*, New York, Penguin Books

Jeffcoate, R (1984) *Ethnic Minorities and Education*, London, Harper and Row

Johnson, P (1992) Assessing the Links, *Junior Education* October 1992.

Keel, P (ed) (1994) *Assessment in the Multi-ethnic Primary Classroom*, Stoke-on-Trent, Trentham Books

Kerr, T and Desforges, M (1988) 'Developing Bilingual Children's English in School' in Verma, G and Pumfrey, P (eds) *Educational Attainments*, Lewes, Falmer Press

Khan, S (1994) Bilingualism and the Curriculum, *Multicultural Teaching*, Vol 13 No 1

Klein, G (1985) *Reading into Racism*, London, Routledge and Kegan Paul

Klein, G (1993) *Education towards Race Equality*, London, Cassell

Kumar, R (1988) Real Books?, *Issues in Race and Education*, No 54

Labov, W (1969) The Logic of Non-standard English, *Georgetown Monographs on Language and Linguistics* Vol 22

Lambert, W (1990) 'Persistent Issues in Bilingualism' in Harley, B et al (eds) *The Development of Second Language Proficiency,* Cambridge, Cambridge University Press

Leung, C (1994) Meeting with SCAA, *Report in Naldic News No 2*, Jan 1994

Leung, C (1995) *Linguistic Diversity in the 1990s; Some Language Education Issues for Minority Ethnic Pupils*, Thames Valley University

Levine, J (ed) (1990) *Bilingual Learners and the Mainstream Curriculum*, Lewes, Falmer Press

Lunzer, E and Gardner, K (eds) (1979) *The Effective Use of Reading,* London, Heinemann

Lunzer, E and Gardner, K (1984) *Learning from the Written Word*, Edinburgh, Oliver and Boyd.

Macdonald, I (1989) *Murder in the Playground*, London, Longsight Press

Marland, M (1977) *Language Across the Curriculum*, London, Heinemann

Martin-Jones, M and Romaine, S (1986) Semilingualism: A Half-Baked Theory of Communicative Competence, *Applied Linguistics* Vol 7 No.1

Mayor, B (1988) 'What does it mean to be bilingual?' in Mercer, N (ed) *Language and Literacy; Language Studies*, Milton Keynes, Open University Press

McGahern, D (1994) Secondary pupils coming new to English and the proposed cuts in Section 11 funds; the importance of Circular 11, *Multicultural Teaching* Vol 12 No 2

McLaughlin, B (1990) 'The relationship between first and second languages; language proficiency and language aptitude' in Harley, B et al *The Development of Second Language Proficiency*, Cambridge, Cambridge University Press

McNiff, J (1993) *Teaching as Learning*, London, Routledge

Mehmet Ali, A (1986) Community Involvement and Accountability as a Question of Power, paper presented to Conference on Issues and Problems of Multi-cultural Societies, Falkenstein, Germany.

Mercer, N (ed) (1981) *Language in School and Community*, London, Edward Arnold

Mercer, N (ed) (1988) *Language and Literacy; Vol 1 Language Studies*, Milton Keynes, Open University Press

Met, M (1994) 'Teaching content through a second language' in Genesee, F (ed) *Educating Second Language Children*, Cambridge,Cambridge University Press

Miller, J (1983) *Many Voices*, London, Routledge and Kegan Paul

Mills, J (1994) 'Finding a voice; bilingual classroom assistants and their role in primary schools' in Blackledge (ed) *Teaching Bilingual Children*, Stoke-on-Trent, Trentham

Mills, R and Mills, J (1993) *Bilingualism in the Primary School*, London, Routledge

Milroy, J and Milroy, L (1985) *Authority in Language*, London, Routledge and Kegan Paul

Ming Tsow, (1986) Dual Language or Not? *Language Matters* No 3

Mobley, M (1987) *Making Ourselves Clearer; Readability in the GCSE*, Secondary Examinations Council

Mohan, B A (1986) *Language and Content*, Reading, M.A, Addison-Wesley

Moon, B Murphy, P and Raynor, J (1989) *Policies for the Curriculum*, London, Hodder and Stoughton

Morrison, M and Sandhu, P (1992) 'Towards a Multilingual Pedagogy' in Norman,K (ed) *Thinking Voices*, London, Hodder and Stoughton

Mortimore, P et al (1988) *School Matters*, Somerset, Open Books

Mullard,C (1982) 'Multiracial Education in Britain:From Assimilation to Cultural Pluralism' in Tierney, J (ed) *Race,Migration and Schooling*, London, Holt,Rinehart and Winston

Murphy, P (1989) 'Gender and Assessment in Science' in Murphy and Moon (eds) *Developments in Learning and Assessment*, London, Hodder and Stoughton

Murphy, P and Moon, B (1989) *Developments in Learning and Assessment*, London, Hodder and Stoughton

National Union of Teachers (1989) *Anti-racism in Education*, London N.U.T.

National Union of Teachers (1992) *Antiracist Curriculum Guidelines*, London, NUT

Norman, K (ed) (1992) *Thinking Voices*, London, Hodder and Stoughton

Novak, J and Gowin, D (1984) *Learning How to Learn*, Cambridge, Cambridge University Press

OFSTED (1993) *Access and Achievement in Urban Education*, London, HMSO

OFSTED (1994) *Handbook for the Inspection of Schools*, London, HMSO

OFSTED (1994) *Educational Support for Minority Ethnic Communities*, London, Office for Standards in Education

OFSTED (1995) *New Framework for the Inspection of Schools*, consultation papers, London, HMSO

Osler, A (1994) 'The Flavour of the Moment? Bilingual Teachers' Experiences of Teaching and

Learning' in Blackledge (ed) *Teaching Bilingual Children,* Stoke-on-Trent, Trentham Books

Patrick, P and Burke, H (1993) 'Equal Opportunities and Sexuality' in Claire, Maybin and Swann *Equality Matters* Clevedon, Multilingual Matters.

Perera, K (1981) 'Some Language Problems in School Learning' in Mercer, N (ed) *Language in School and Community*, London, Edward Arnold

Perera, K (1986) 'Some linguistic difficulties in school textbooks' in Gillham, B (ed) *The Language of School Subjects*, London, Heinemann

Perera, K (1987) *Understanding Language*, National Association for Advisors in English

Pinsent, P (1992) *Language, Culture and Young Children*, London, David Fulton

Pollard, A and Tann, S (1987) *Reflective Teaching in the Primary School*, London, Cassell

Preiswerk, R (ed) (1980) *The Slant of the Pen*, Geneva, World Council of Churches

Refugee Council (undated) *Helping Refugee Children in Schools*, London, Refugee Council

Reid, J-A, Forrestal, P and Cook, J (1989) *Small Group Learning in the Classroom*, Australia, Chalkface Press

Richardson, R (1990) *Daring to be a Teacher*, Stoke-on-Trent, Trentham Books

Richmond, J and Savva, H (1983) *Investigating Our Language*, London, Edward Arnold

Rivera, C (ed)(1984) *Language Proficiency and Academic Achievement,* Clevedon, Multilingual Matters

Robinson, B (1985) 'Bilingualism and Mother-tongue Maintenance in Britain' in Brumfit et al (eds) *English as a Second Language in the United Kingdom*, Oxford, Pergamon Press

Robson, A (1986) Bilingual learners – school based assessment, *Gnosis* 10

Romaine, S (1984) *The Language of Children and Adolescents*, Oxford, Basil Blackwell

Romaine, S (1989) *Bilingualism*, Oxford, Blackwell

Rosen, H and Burgess, T (1980) *Languages and Dialects of London School Children*, London, Ward Lock Educational

Runnymede Trust (1993) *Equality Assurance in Schools*, Stoke-on-Trent, Trentham Books

Rutter, J (1994) *Refugee Children in the Classroom*, Stoke-on-Trent, Trentham Books

Sallis, J (1994) *Free for All?* London, The Campaign for State Education

Sarup, M (1986) *The Politics of Multiracial Education*, London,Routledge and Kegan Paul

Savva, H (1990) 'The Rights of Bilingual Children' in Carter (ed) *Knowledge About Language*, London, Hodder and Stoughton.

Schon, D (1983) *The Reflective Practitioner*, London, Temple-Smith

Shan, S-J (1990) Assessment by monolingual teachers of developing bilinguals at Key Stage 1, *Multicultural Teaching* Vol 9 No 1

Shan, S-J and Bailey, P (1991) *Multiple Factors*, Stoke-on-Trent,Trentham Books

Sidhu, B (1993) 'Teachers speak out' in Mills, R and J (eds)*Bilingualism in the Primary School*, London, Routledge

Siraj-Blatchford,I (1994) Some practical strategies for collaboration between parents and Early Years educators, *Multicultural Teaching*, Vol 12 No 2

Skutnabb-Kangas, T (1981) *Bilingualism or Not*, Clevedon, Multilingual Matters

Skutnabb-Kangas, T and Cummins, J (eds) (1988) *Minority Education*, Clevedon, Multilingual Matters.

Smith, D and Tomlinson, S (1989) *The School Effect; A study of multi-racial comprehensives*, London, Policy Studies Institute

Stenhouse, L (1975) *An Introduction to Curriculum Research and Development*, Oxford, Heinemann Educational

Stenhouse, L Verma, G Wild, R and Nixon, J (1982) *Teaching about Race Relation: Problems and Effects*, London, Routledge and Kegan Paul

Stinton, J (1979) *Racism and Sexism in Children's Books*, London, Writers and Readers

Stone, M (1981) *The Education of the Black Child in Britain*, London, Collins Fontana

Stubbs, M (ed) (1985) *The Other Languages of England*, London, Routledge and Kegan Paul

Sturman, E (1988) 'Zeynep: That Really Happened to Me' in CUES Collaborative Learning Group (eds) *Collaborative Learning*, London, CUES

Sutton, C (ed) (1981) *Communicating in the Classroom*, Hodder and Stoughton

Swann, J (1993) 'Assessing Language' in Claire, Maybin and Swann (eds) *Equality Matters*, Clevedon, Multilingual Matters

Task Group on Assessment and Testing (1987) *Report,* London, DES

Tierney, J (ed) (1982) *Race, Migration and Schooling*, London,Holt,Rinehart and Winston

Tizard, B and Hughes, M (1984) *Young Children Learning*, London, Fontana Press

Thorp, S (ed) (1991) *Race, Equality and Science Teaching*, Association for Science Education

Tonjes, M (1986) 'Reading and thinking skills required in the subject classroom' in Gillham (ed) *The Language of School Subjects*, London, Heinemann

Tosi, A (1988) 'The Jewel in the Crown of the Modern Prince' in Skutnabb-Kangas, T and Cummins, J (eds) *Minority Education*, Clevedon, Multilingual Matters

Troyna, B (ed) (1987) *Racial Inequality in Education*, London, Tavistock

Troyna, B (1989) 'Beyond Multiculturalism; Towards the Enactment of Antiracist Education in Policy, Provision and Pedagogy' in Moon, B Murphy, P and Raynor, J *Policies for the Curriculum*, London, Hodder and Stoughton

Twitchin, J (ed) (1988) *The Black and White Media Book*, Stoke-on-Trent, Trentham Books

Verma, G and Pumfrey, P (eds) (1988) *Educational Attainments*, Lewes, Falmer Press

Waheed, S (1992) 'The Two Worlds of Language' in Bain et al (eds) *Looking into Language,* London, Hodder and Stoughton.

Webb, R (ed) (1990) *Practitioner Research in the Primary School*, Lewes, Falmer Press

Wells, G (1986) *The Meaning Makers*, London, Hodder and Stoughton

Wells, G and Nicholls, J (eds) (1985) *Language and Learning; an Interactional Perspective*, Lewes, Falmer Press

Whitehead, M (1990) *Language and Literacy in the Early Years*, London, Paul Chapman

Widdowson, H (1979) *Reading and Thinking in English*, Oxford, Oxford University Press

Wilkins, D.A (1976) *Notional Syllabuses,* Oxford, Oxford University Press

Wiles, S (1981) 'Language Issues in the Multi-cultural Classroom' in Mercer,N (ed) *Language in School and Community*, London, Edward Arnold

Wiles, S (1985) Learning a Second Language, *English Magazine*, No 14

Wong Fillmore, L (1980) *Language Learning Through Bilingual Instruction*, Berkeley, University of California

Wong Fillmore, L (1991) 'Second-language learning in children; a model of language learning in social context' in Bialystok (ed) *Language Processing in Bilingual Children*, Cambridge, Cambridge University Press.

Wood, D (1988) *How Children Think and Learn*, Oxford, Basil Blackwell

Wright, C (1985) The Influence of School Processes on the Educational Opportunities of Children of West Indian Origin, *Multicultural Teaching*, Vol 4 No 1

Wright, C (1987) 'Black students – White teachers' in Troyna, B (ed) *Racial Inequality in Education*, London Tavistock

Wright, J (1982)) *Bilingualism in Education*, London, CUES

Zaslavsky, C (1979) *Africa Counts*, New York, Lawrence Hill

Index